SUCCESS

Prentice Hall
BUSINESS

Books to make you better

Books to make you better. To make you *be* better, *do* better, *feel* better. Whether you want to upgrade your personal skills or change your job, whether you want to improve your managerial style, become a more powerful communicator, or be stimulated and inspired as you work.

Prentice Hall Business is leading the field with a new breed of skills, careers and development books. Books that are a cut above the mainstream – in topic, content and delivery – with an edge and verve that will make you better, with less effort.

Books that are as sharp and smart as you are.

Prentice Hall Business.
We work harder – so you don't have to.

For more details on products, and to contact us, visit
www.pearsoned.co.uk

SUCCESS

RICHARD HALL

**THE NEED TO SUCCEED IS IN YOUR GENES
THE WAY TO SUCCEED IS IN THIS BOOK**

PEARSON
Prentice Hall
BUSINESS

Harlow, England • London • New York • Boston • San Francisco • Toronto
Sydney • Tokyo • Singapore • Hong Kong • Seoul • Taipei • New Delhi
Cape Town • Madrid • Mexico City • Amsterdam • Munich • Paris • Milan

PEARSON EDUCATION LIMITED

Edinburgh Gate
Harlow CM20 2JE
Tel: +44 (0)1279 623623
Fax: +44 (0)1279 431059
Website: www.pearsoned.co.uk

First published in Great Britain in 2005

ISBN 0 273 69369 7

British Library Cataloguing-in-Publication Data
A catalogue record for this book is available from the British Library

Library of Congress Cataloging-in-Publication Data
A catalog record for this book is available from the Library of Congress

10 9 8 7 6 5 4 3 2 1
09 08 07 06 05

Typeset in 15pt Minion by 30
Printed and bound by Bell & Bain Limited, Glasgow

The Publisher's policy is to use paper manufactured from sustainable forests

Acknowledgements

After Gwyneth Paltrow and then Sarah Jessica Parker the vogue for the extravagant 'thank you' has, perhaps, come under question.

That's why this is brief.

Thank you Kate, my wife, for typing the manuscript and making helpful comments.

Thank you to all the contributors and especially to the insightful thoughts of John Neill of Unipart.

Thank you Mike Horne, Martin Conradi, Crispin Manners, Alison Chesney. The inspiring and interesting leaders with whom I work.

Thank you to all those I mentor who teach me so much more than they imagine.

And thank you the Pearson team. You have been supportive, thorough and great fun. Especially you Rachael Stock.

All of you have been hugely successful yourselves in helping me see how success works.

Contents

Fast Foreword

SUCCESS – THE MICROWAVED QUICK-READ VERSION

People ask me if this is a 'how to' book.

Although I deeply loathe the idea of 'how to' business books in the same way I hate table d'hôte menus – too little choice in advice and what there is is left over from someone else's yesterdays – I have to confess that this is at its heart a 'how to' book.

But it's a 'how to' book with a difference.

It's also a 'why to' and a 'what to' book.

It examines what success is today to different people and it also considers different levels of success. Better, I'd argue, to be a happily successful specialist at middle-ranking level than a flawed, inadequate and ultimately unsuccessful CEO (even if you envy his trappings of success – 'but you should see his car!' – you need to beware the downsides – 'his cholesterol and his life expectancy'.)

The menu of 'how to's' that you can choose from is long. But everyone is different. There are no formulaic quick fixes and you are much better off with a long list of 'try this' tips than a table d'hôte prescription such as that in the best-selling book *The One Minute Manager* (powerful as this may seem, even if it's just for one minute.)

Because there's so much in the book I've included two blank pages at the end marked 1–10 with the legend *The Ten Most Useful Success Ideas I've Found in this Book.*

Fill it in when you've read, skipped through, speed read or dipped in and out of the book.

If you take out ten ideas I'll be delighted, and my guess is you'll be en route to being a lot more successful as well.

To help you through the book here are *my* ten most important things for you to think about before you start reading it.

1. Success has never been more accessible. We don't have closed shops like we used to. If you really *want* to you can succeed. It's hard work but you can do it. How to is in these pages.

2. For some success means money, for others power, for others respect, for others fame, for others ease of mind. You define it. You go for it. The *only* crime is sitting back and doing nothing. And one other thing: the fattest cats don't purr any louder than the sleekest ones.

3. How you use your time is the key to success. And if you go on a Time Management course I'll beat you to death with your Palm Pilot. What you must learn to do is create 'Time Profit' – time you save to spend on stuff you need to do. Do it by shaving time off all you do. Five minutes an hour saved equals nearly an hour and a half in a normal day.

4. Do not punish yourself by trying to *finish* everything you do. Be happy to *complete* things. That is, do them in the time you have and on time. No, it's not about relaxing standards – it's being realistic about how long it takes to get what needs to be done done *on time*, that's all. Too much to do means you just get done what you can as brilliantly as you able – just as you did in exams.

5. Look at yourself honestly – brutally honestly. Take stock. Go on an improvement regime from top to bottom. Give yourself targets and tasks. Amazingly, the biggest confidence booster is feeling good about yourself. Surprisingly, being in better shape helps do this.

6. Become a 'Grand Inquisitor'. Ask 'why' a lot. Look at everything from every angle. Take nothing for granted. Don't accept things you aren't happy with. Do not let anyone bulls*** you.

7. Become enormously curious about what is going on around you. Read like reading is about to be banned. *Hear* what people are saying – that's more effective than just listening. *See* what's going on – that's more effective than just looking. Get out there in the street, into stores, with people who actually buy things. In other words, 'get real' and stop what I call 'air-conditioned thinking' (that's what they do at the top of ivory towers).

8. Be a team player. This is not about YOU. It's about a team because synergy works – it really does. Do all you can to create the best team around you and the people with whom you can create the best things. Be ruthless in few things but this. Get rid of anything and anyone who stops your team performing well together, however great they might be as individuals.

9. Work harder. Yes, I know … impossible … unreasonable … unfair. All successes in whatever walk of life have more energy, more get-up-and-go, than the average. They have an appetite for life. For getting up and getting out. They may feel tired, they don't act tired. They are 'doers'. They are 'completers'. And they don't stop till they've got it done.

10. Love what you do. Enthusiasm is amazing and infectious stuff. It makes you feel good and realize just how horrible cynics are to sit next to at dinner, at meetings, at anything. Life will not always deal you a great hand but the resounding impact of a 'let's make the best of this' brings out the best in everyone. There's one other thing. You have to spend so much time with yourself; how much better to spend it with someone inspiring, enthusiastic and cheerful.

Introduction

In the mid 1980s a new product was launched in Japan. It was an immediate success. Called 'Succeed', it was a pill that contained a mix of caffeine and vitamins.

It was aimed at teenage students. The caffeine was to keep them awake. The vitamins were to keep them alive.

Yes, that's how seriously they and their parents took preparing for exams. One poor chap who failed his exams decided to saw his head off. His neighbours thought this represented such a feat of courage as to excuse his exam failure.

Although I take the idea of success pretty seriously (I shouldn't be writing this book otherwise), I don't go as far as this.

At least, not quite.

When the need to succeed becomes obsessive, when it gets in the way of everything else, it's time to call a truce.

It's good to succeed – by which I mean progressing, achieving goals, reaching what you want to reach. But it's critical you don't take it or yourself too seriously.

Success is good. No – it's better than good, it's great. Great in the same way it's great seeing young children embarking on the discovery of learning. The thrill of success is in that momentum, that invincibility of spirit that is quite simply about being a player, a contender. Success lifts the spirits.

The oft-quoted American Football coach Henry 'Red' Sanders said: 'Sure, winning isn't everything. It's the only thing.'

Half of me says, 'Enough, Red – go back to your cheerleaders'. The other half is secretly applauding the sheer feistiness of his claim.

Triumph, like disaster, Rudyard Kipling told us, is an 'imposter'. But the trouble with this Old Britain icon is he seemed to secretly enjoy losing. Liked cold showers and that kind of stuff too. Not very PC. Certainly not a man of today.

To be sure, in the scheme of things personal success in business will hardly make any celestial headlines. Few of us on our deathbed are likely to mutter valedictory words like 'I managed to increase the brand share …' or 'I wish I'd worked harder and gone to more meetings.'

Life is a glorious game and part of the game rules of life is to do one's very best to make the most of those amazing talents you were born with. You didn't realize you were amazing? Well, realize it now. Unless *you* think you are great, no one else will.

Success is when things work out better than we'd hoped and failure is when things don't work out as we'd hoped or expected. But failure is not disaster. Indeed, it's from failure that we frequently learn our most useful lessons. Failure is very often the springboard for great success.

The book is focused on ways of increasing the chance of succeeding. It's about reducing those handicaps that make someone with potential stumble or take longer than they should to realize their talents.

It's about self-discovery.

It's about building your own tool kit with which to fashion success.

It's about heightening the buzz you get at work.

It's about having more fun.

It's about getting promoted.

It's about earning more money.

It's about being as great as you can be.

But do you really want to succeed? Or do you just want to be quite successful and very happy? Do you want to define success in your terms? Or do you want to be effective at getting results but an unlikeable bastard – the person whose departure from his company provokes wild celebration?

Alternatively, do you want people around you to regard you as a success and like you for it ('all that success hasn't spoilt him or her').

Success.

Try it. It's fun. It's exciting. I really think you are going to like it. A lot.

'I have learned that everyone wants to live on the peak of the mountain without knowing that the real happiness is in how it is scaled.'

Gabriel García Márquez

'Always make sure your bow wave is bigger than your wake.'

Sir Mark Weinberg when CEO of Allied Hambro

1 What is Success?

One of those things which seems pretty straightforward until you start analyzing it and then you really start to worry.

But don't worry – success is like oxygen – it keeps you going.

'Don't think too big, don't think too small, don't think too much.'

Control Data advertisement

WHAT ACTUALLY IS SUCCESS?

Have you ever really sat down and thought about it? Do so now for two minutes.

It's not that simple is it?

When first challenged nearly all of us can describe success easily. Michael Winner, for instance, seems to have no problem with it. Success to him seems to be living in Mayfair, having a chauffeur-driven car, eating good food (lots of it) in fine restaurants and having lots of money. That's what he says in his much-reviled and even more read column on restaurants in the *Sunday Times*. Success described like this is precisely why Michael Winner is regarded by some, it would seem by the letters he receives in *The Sunday Times* for which he writes, as an extravagant showoff, moneybags and self-centred parvenu. But anyone who brought you *Winner's Dinners*, *Death Wish* and 'calm down dear it's only a commercial' deserves our applause. Whatever else he is you can't deny he's a success. Michael

Moore is much the same. Famous films. Famous waistline. Famous ego. Famously successful.

It's not easy defining success because it means different things to different people. To some it is about money, to some it is about power, to some it is about gaining respect, to some it is about winning, to some it is about doing something that would be regarded as meaning something (a vicar, a social worker or whatever – successful? You bet – you need to see the work they do to understand this.) To a few it is about gaining immortality.

I saw a poster recently with Benjamin Franklin's words on how to be remembered, 'do something worth writing about or write something worth reading'. Chilling words to any writer but overall good advice if, indeed, it's the marble of immortality you want.

Let's go through the options.

Money?

Yes, that would be nice, or so most people seem to think. Useful stuff that gives you choices. What you buy, where you live, what you drive. To many, choice is the greatest wealth they aspire to. Listen to anyone talking about winning the lottery and it's the things they'd choose to do with the money that absorbs them. Intriguingly, most of them talk winsomely about the *good* things they'd do with the money. Given half a chance, most people would display a very strong philanthropic streak.

So, no question, the display of wealth is an important signal of success. But money alone is not enough. Indeed, too much money is not seen as good at all and being described as a 'fat cat' is as insulting as you can get.

Seeing CEOs earn over £1 million a year has become commonplace now. Breathtaking sums of money are earned or secured through share deals. The world is full of very rich people – very successful people, though? I'm not so sure. Nor are many others.

Interestingly, Rocco Forte, the ex-CEO of Forte Hotels who was trounced by Granada in a takeover battle of the mid 1990s and lost his family empire, has recreated a new hotel chain in a different way. He seems both successful and happy – a conjunction that seems increasingly important to people I've discussed this with. He's happy because he's doing what he's best at: creating luxury hotels. He's successful because he's survived and is getting on with his life. His opinion of the one-time successful Granada team Gerry Robinson and Charles Allen (once both fêted as the 'darlings of the City' – ooh, how the mighty are fallen) is predictably acerbic: 'They're both failures.' In terms of wealth creation for themselves, clearly not. Understandable sour grapes, perhaps. But he has a point. Forte still means something in the hotel world. Granada? No, probably not.

The money issue is dramatically highlighted by Michael Moore in his lively outpouring *Dude, Where's My Country?* The darling and prizewinner of Cannes, democrat, American eccentric and apparently a bit of a handful, he nonetheless writes a diverting critique of the Bush administration and comes up with this astounding statistic about the relative pay of a CEO and an average worker in a company.

To be sure this has been the subject of a lot of debate recently and in Canada they're talking about introducing legislation to ensure the multiple does not exceed ten. Faint hope. It's thirteen in Scandinavia, sixteen in Germany and twenty-four in 'fat-cat Britain'. So how do the Americans fare?

In the USA it's – I pause for breath – four hundred and eleven. Looks better in words so I'll do it in numbers. *411*. And for effect, one more time … *411*. So if the average worker earns $20,000, the average CEO earns $8,200,000.

Now that's what I call successful. That's a real redistribution of wealth … to those that already have it. Until recently the acquisition of great wealth in the United States seemed OK, part of the American dream, a goal to which everyone could aspire.

Being successfully rich is beginning to mean seriously overloaded with barrel-loads of money. *Frankly, it's a bit embarrassing.*

But money gives you *power* doesn't it?

Not necessarily.

In Charles Handy's *The New Alchemists* the first of these magicians that he's chosen is William Atkinson, headmaster of the Phoenix High School.

I know William. He is what they call a 'Superhead'. That means a senior headmaster parachuted in to save an ailing or failing school. He's amazing. Energetic, passionate, opinionated, full of life and laughter. Quite simply he makes Lenny Henry (who, it is rumoured, based some of his act on William) look a docile, slow-talking, reflective chap in comparison.

William is *successful*. Self-evidently. He has access to all the ears in government (and even if he didn't have those ears he'd seize them anyway and he wouldn't take 'no' for an answer). But I doubt (I don't know and I wouldn't ask) if he is really wealthy, not wealthy in the fat-cat sense at any rate.

He is, however, powerful. Powerful in that he's really well known, respected and wired in to those who supposedly wield power and hold the levers of government. He has also a special kind of power beyond that – the power to do good and to change opinion. On this, he is self-deprecating: 'They [the people in real power] listen. Sure they listen. I think they actually agree but in the event nothing much usually happens. Until we have a crisis and then the money comes flooding in. We always get the money then. But it's always late and because of that so much less effective than it could have been if it had come when we needed it first.'

William is successful on two counts. The *power* he has (even though actually making things happen seems sometimes frustratingly slow – even prime ministers find this) and the *respect* in which he's held.

The '*respect* issue' is an interesting one. Everyone wants it. Yet money alone can't buy it for you. Imagine poor Gerald Ronson's vision of respect as he saw it – Lord Ronson of Marylebone – evaporate in front of his eyes as he became embroiled in the Guinness share-price-fixing scandal of the mid 1980s when they were trying to take over Distillers. Not just embroiled, actually imprisoned. In retrospect the offence seems pretty mild (if offence it was) compared with the sleazemongers of a decade later and what they all got up to.

It's pretty clear that Tom Peters prizes respect above money or power in his book *Re-imagine!* in which he speculates about the kind of epitaph he would most like to have. Not for him any passive 'he did his best' stuff. He wants 'Tom Peters. He was a player'.

Not bad, Tom. But not as good as Ernest Hemingway:

> *'Put a bottle at my feet and one at my head and if I don't drink it you'll know that I'm dead.'*

Tom clearly wants peer-group respect. And don't we all? Isn't one incontrovertible definition of success quite simply winning the hearts, minds and votes of those around us? Understand that and you understand the sheer adrenalin surge of being a politician in a democracy at election time.

The success that comes from *winning* is easy to understand. Sports psychology is pretty simple stuff really. In fact, it baffles me that companies invite Olympic sprinters to their management conferences believing that in so doing their experiences or, rather, the rationalizations of their experiences, composed for just such audiences, will in fact inspire or change their executives. We've all heard it:

> *'Get into the Zone … the Zone is being in that very centre of yourself where it is quiet apart from the applause of the certainty that you are going to win … you are going to run this race backwards … you are raising your arms in triumph … now zone yourself back to the start and believe it is true.'*

Executives nod sagely at each other. This feels so familiar (they lie to each other), so at one with their day-to-day experience, so good to talk about in the pub on Saturday.

Winning by stretching your own body and preventing that most dangerous melon-sized lump getting in the way (i.e. your brain) is meat and drink to an athlete. Managing a business, running a team, solving a business problem, living your life – none of these bear any relation to the business of althleticism.

No relation? Well, yes – there are exceptions. There are parallel relationships in team sports but they're limited. The number of times I've heard people trying to draw analogies between the English World Champion

Rugby team and business is extraordinary. But, sorry guys, it's a flawed analogy except in so far as preparation, planning, practice, communication, team spirit and so on are common to both. Tell Alan Leighton that running the Post Office is like running a rugby team and he'll tell you to get stuffed. In that respect and that alone he does resemble a rugby player. We'll talk about Sir Clive Woodward later. It's the caring about the tiny details that's a lesson to us all. It's also, of course, not just about winning but winning again and again. Sir Clive should talk to Arsene Wenger about this one.

And yet 'winning' does constitute one of the ingredients of success for most people. Winning not so much in the sports sense but in the 'winning formula' sense. You hear people in business talk about 'being on a roll', which more appetisingly translated means having all their biorhythms working in synchronization, being at one with themselves, being supremely self-confident. I described this sensation to an American friend of mine, Teresa Ceballos, who heads up the marketing at Leapfrog, the rapidly growing global toy business, as 'feeling invincible'. She took issue with this, saying the word 'invincible' was too harshly militaristic for her taste. Well, I still disagree. Maybe it's a language thing where American and English part company, but I think feeling invincible is just great. Strangely, Teresa and I seldom disagree – she's a true success. Feisty, fun, effective. A 'do it, do it' person. Momentum is her middle name. And I think she's invincible.

Confused?

You should be. We've hardly scratched the surface yet. Success is relative to the culture in which it occurs and within a limited time span. From hero to zero in a few months. From champ to chump.

Being a success in India – an executive in a call centre – would hardly raise a ripple of applause in the UK. Yet look at some of the realities of that new job. Mike Kirsch, Operations Director of Norwich Union, talks about the development of new call centres in India:

'We're building new offices. They're all air-conditioned. They have 24/7 canteens and TV rooms. Working there carries real prestige. They're all graduates. The money is poor by our standards but it's three times what an Indian GP gets.'

It sounds wonderful – *relatively*. Best of all, their colleagues are all very bright and, like you, hungry for success (that word again). The working conditions themselves confer status on the job. Ever wonder why the world's largest banks insist on such impressive working monuments? It gives them prestige. It allows your workers to be (literally if you are, for instance, in the HSBC building at Canary Wharf) *above* your peers.

Success to someone young and to someone more mature in years will probably be different things. To the former the goal of immediate pro-motion and more-money-than-you-need salary is potentially a driver. I recall saying (could I really have been so gauche?) to a young employee years ago, 'Look, if you haven't made it by the time you're 30 you're stuffed' (and no, I don't play rugby either) and yet I was in advertising, and if you look at what's happening nowadays in marketing services and at the ages of key executives I was right – I may have been a nasty piece of materialistic work but, nonetheless, right. When you are young patience is not a virtue. *You want it now and you want it in technicolor.*

It's that very desire, that very hunger for achievement, that makes this age group so appealing and so important to shareholders. They are 'make it happen' people. They have energy and they haven't made as many mis-takes as older people with all the fear that that brings. Listen to an older sportsman talk about the flush of young don't-care-just-go-for-it bravado (McEnroe, Jacklin, Botham, Woods). Experience is great stuff but it isn't on a par with the appetite that doing it for the first time generates.

So what success is depends on how you look at it, where you started, what's expected of you, what your peers are doing, but most of all what makes you happy.

And if you are beginning to think a relatively simple word like 'success' is in fact complicated then you should try 'happy'. We really are treading on eggshells and straying into Professor Joad country. Joad was a philosopher who became famous on a radio programme called the *Brains Trust* (the precursor to *Any Questions*) by his frequently repeated line, 'It all depends what you mean by …'

This same Joad described the dilemma of trying to attain happiness like this:

> *'My life is spent in a perpetual alternation between two rhythms, the rhythm of attracting people for fear I may be lonely, and the rhythm of trying to get rid of them because I know I am bored.'*

The rhythm of success and happiness is about as tortured. It strays between the adrenalin of achievement and the guilt of self-absorption, the satisfaction of peer-group applause and the dismay that it is all transitory and that no one is irreplaceable.

Ultimately, success in business for most of us is relatively easy to achieve provided we limit our ambition to what is achievable and not the stuff of some wildly improbable dream – remember Michael Palin in *Monty Python* and the 'I want to be a lion tamer' sketch? What he *thought* he wanted and *actually* wanted were miles apart. Entrepreneurs may disagree with this but there are few of these around and they tend to be highly individualistic – or do I mean mad?

Success in life is harder to achieve and to define. My own version goes like this:

> *'We are born with certain assets and abilities. It is our duty to make the most of these, to develop them and to use them. And when we die it would be good if those around us could say "he or she did their best and really made a difference". Better still if they could say "they changed lots of things for the better… and they made life more fun for us all". Perhaps that's asking too much but anything less seems like falling short of our potential.'*

Success is more fun that the alternative. And it's honestly easier to achieve than you might think. *If you really try. And if you have a plan.*

2 Succeed Without Taking Yourself too Seriously

It's natural to want to succeed. It goes back to childhood. We all have a survival and a success instinct. It's just that we sometimes forget how to exploit it. And it's just that we take it and ourselves far too seriously.

'People who reach the top of the tree are only those who haven't got the qualifications to detain them at the bottom.'

Peter Ustinov

I'M THE KING OF THE CASTLE

That's the battlecry of the successful child. Success is a natural goal for most people. Watch children playing and the basic instincts of territorialism, acquisition and their assertion of will are obvious. They actually play to win, to achieve success.

The debate about what success is and whether it is good or bad is a relatively recent thing. Civilized society tends to move from the need to survive to the need to succeed to the need to debate (too much of this in life right now) ... what generally follows is decadence and decline: Rome, Greece, Venice, the British Empire.

William James (Henry's brother) showed great vitriol nearly a century ago. His words will ring true to many today:

'The moral flabbiness born of the exclusive worship of the bitch-goddess success. That – with the squalid cash interpretation put on the word success – is our national disease.'

Well, I love the anger; he's almost spluttering with rage. I should really have called this book *Bitch-goddess* to maximize its sales success and its 'squalid cash interpretation'. William has more vigour than his cerebral brother. But is he right?

To most who are on the so-called 'ladder' (whether it be a property ladder, career ladder, marriage ladder or simply the ladder of life) almost certainly not. Once we've had our fill we can afford to renounce the 'bitch-goddess'. Until then we are, most of us, up, running and energized.

You can try to take success away. The PC approach to one primary school beating another at football 29–0 was to ban anyone winning more than 15–0 or even, extreme liberal wing, eliminating the score altogether. It could, I suppose, catch on in professional sport: 'Arsenal and Manchester United played superb and exciting football. Well done both teams.'

Robin Marlar rather surprisingly took against the 'win at all costs' ethic of, for instance, the Australians at cricket:

'Why play if not to win? For fun, for friendship, for experience, to explore.' (The Times, 6 April 2004.*)*

For friendship? Arsene Wenger, meet Alex Ferguson. Now that was a fun experience boys, wasn't it? No. I can't see it really catching on.

Colin Montgomerie is a golfer. A good one. His marriage break-up made him question what success was and what life was all about. Anyway, he noted recently that if most businessmen he'd played with in pro-ams had the same risk/reward attitude to business that they had to golf they'd go bankrupt very fast.

One of the greatest golfers who ever lived, Bobby Jones, had three maxims we could all afford to adopt to our benefit:

1. Be prepared to make mistakes.

2. Always select shots that have the largest margin of error.

3. Expect some scrambling – it's normal.

Although the need to succeed seems greater in men than in women – would any man say what my wife said as I went to play golf with our daughter's fiancé? 'Be nice to Paul. Let him win' – my wife would argue that this demonstrates how men are defective in not seeing the distinction between winning and success – 'sometimes you have to let the other person, like a child for instance, win so they learn.' That's plausible, I snap, but can I get on? Thanks. As I was saying, the urge of women to succeed in the same way that men succeed is increasing. Look at female golfers playing in men's tournaments. Look at the Williams sisters. Look at Marjorie Scardino. Look at Dianne Thompson. Look at the next generation.

Letting the other guy win is not what we 'Kings of the Castle' can easily do (maybe this is a weakness of egocentricity). *We need to try. We need to win.* Even when the odds are stacked against us we still need to try to overcome them.

This competitive urge is impossible to change. We are born with an instinct to improve. Our lives are built around a desire to find something we are really good at. Those of us who are lucky find that thing, be it business, sport, singing, art, writing, collecting stuff.

Peter Katz, ex-doyen of the toy industry and then importer of high-class kitchen equipment, is a world-leading collector of and expert in toothpicks … 'and ear wax spoons', he eagerly adds. Peter is a world-class success and expert in this niche area.

There was a great line I heard recently: 'If it doesn't matter who wins why do we keep score?' From an early age we have this vision, some of us, of a divine scorer marking off our pluses and minuses in life. Success = heaven. Failure = hell. And don't worry too much if it's the latter and you have a George Burns attitude to life. He said, 'If at first you don't succeed then maybe failure's your thing.'

This *need* to succeed sits right at the top of Maslow's hierarchy – the 'self-actualization' apex. He argues that satisfying the needs (physiological, safety, love, esteem) is healthy … we are all of us 'needs junkies' with cravings that must be satisfied. Self-actualization is defined as follows: '*The desire to become more and more what one is, to become everything that one is capable of becoming.*'

The need to succeed is a major driver to progress in civilized society. It only becomes dangerous when the need becomes totally obsessive and self-absorbing. It only becomes a problem when the need to *succeed* is overtaken by the need to satisfy *greed*.

For examples of what happens to people whose need to succeed becomes immoderate, refer to Macbeth or any other Shakespearian or Jacobean villain. Their bloodstained corpses line the world's stages.

The greatest aid to self-perspective I know is retaining one's sense of humour. Perhaps I should rename this book *The Need to Succeed without Taking Yourself too Seriously*. It's interesting how many pundits and gurus call business a 'game'. Games, although deadly serious while they last, are, when all's said and done, just games or interludes in the more serious stuff of life.

3 Success is an Attitude of Mind

Success is available to everyone, it really is, if only you can get in the right frame of mind. You only need to be awake, sober and positive (and I'm not really sure about sober).

'A man can stand anything except a succession of ordinary days.'

Goethe

'Success is a science; if you have the conditions you get the result.'

Oscar Wilde, 1883

'True success is to labour.'

Robert Louis Stevenson
(Virginibus Puerisque 1881)

EIGHT INCHES TO SUCCESS

How can it be, I asked Ian Parker, CEO of Privilege Insurance, that to many people moving-ball games seemed easier than still-ball games? Thinking about it, how can anyone find golf difficult? Described simply, it seems so straightforward. Yet even without an opponent, playing by yourself on a beautiful day on an easy course in a good mood, how can it be you are in the rough, in bunkers, playing shanks off perfect lies, topping tee shots and missing two-foot putts?

I'd suggest it was sabotage.

And of course, in a way, it is.

Do you remember a film with Woody Allen called *Everything You always Wanted to Know about Sex (and Were Afraid to Ask)* and the saboteur who infiltrates the 'conscience room' and is destroying the sex drive? I'm convinced there's a guilty infiltrator in my brain whenever I play golf. An insidious, slimy little fellow who mutters stuff like 'Go on miss it, it's only a game', 'All coordination systems collapse on the cry of three – 1, 2, 3 – shank', 'Faster, faster – go on – you can swing much faster than that'.

Ed Smith's book on cricket describes it as a *weak voice* (that's the cringing 'I can't do it' voice) and a *strong voice* (that's 'I'm invincible, me'). Well, he did get a double first but for me this is just too complex.

We have a sense of oneness when we're on song.

We feel lucky

We feel cool

We feel powerful

We feel one step ahead

We feel nimble and fast on our feet

We have breadth of vision (literally – our peripheral vision improves)

We feel as though we are right

I call it a sense of '*calm invincibility*'.

We all know the reverse when quite simply we feel clumsy and slow.

And what's involved in moving from one to the other is the eight inches between our ears. Electricity in there flicks the 'can do switch'. There's also a 'divert switch' you've got to flick first that can take us round that squodgy bit in our mind called 'self-doubt'.

To flick that tricky little switch try the following medicines.

1.   Enthuse, enrapture and enjoy

You need plenty of this whatever you do. It comes from the 'laughter' plant and is distilled with a cocktail of 'fascination' and 'pleasure'.

Quite simply, enjoy what you do.

Often people say they don't much like what they do because they just haven't tried to enjoy it. Say to yourself 'this is great' or 'what are the things about this I enjoy?'

Whatever the job is it can be fun.

I was served by a guy called Greg at Argos in Brighton – he was brilliant, professional, knowledgeable, very fast. I hope he gets promoted. I asked him if he liked what he does. 'I love it. Brilliant. Best job I've ever had.' I could imagine him reading the Argos catalogue in bed ensuring he was word perfect.

He was good at his job because he liked it.

And it also works the other way – he liked his job because he was good at it.

The guys who serve coffee off the trolleys on the Brighton Express seem to be more modern catering pros than old-fashioned British Rail employees. More importantly, they seem to love what they do.

Postmen (or 'posties', as they now call them) are often urbane, intelligent and, when they are good – which they usually are – they are genuinely interested. There's one I know near Newquay who says it's a fabulous job: 'Open air, lots of people, you feel you make a difference'. He described rescuing an old lady trapped in her bath – 'it was part of the job' – and one was overwhelmed by the fact that this was more than an ordinary do-it-leave-it job. It was a social mission.

The very focused Tom Hings, Brand Director at Royal Mail, has produced advertising that tells the more-to-it-than-delivering-a-letter story with great passion. Another guy who loves his job.

It's these people who tell me how much they love what they do that turn me on. It really doesn't matter what they do. Brain surgeon or postman. It's the enjoyment they get that is exciting.

And what do you do if you don't like what you do? There are three things.

1. Change it – life's too short.

2. Analyze why you don't like it and change your attitude towards it.

3. Focus on the things you like and do best and bring them to the job. If you are a great talker, do it instead of emailing. Play to your strengths.

2. Master, expert, king of success

This book is unequivocally in praise of effort and work. Not for it the assumption that success comes easy nor that it belongs to an elite born to it. Today we live in a much more sensible, meritocratic world. One in which those who deserve most will tend to get it. Masters of the Universe twenty-first-century style are those who learn, really learn, their craft be it law, advertising, accountancy, architecture, plumbing, fashion design, marketing, whatever.

Think of every job as being a little like that of being a taxi driver. Sorry, you really do have to do the 'knowledge'. In fact, it wouldn't be so stupid an idea to take a big, black, lined book inscribed on the front:

THE KNOWLEDGE

and insert all you know/don't know, have learned, tips you've picked up and the *learning* programme you've set yourself over the next twelve months.

Am I making this all sound rather hard work?

I espouse perspiration ahead of inspiration, and think if and only if you perspire do you get inspired. The world is changing so rapidly – you can't operate by instinct alone. You have got to be on a constant learning curve. You have to develop your knowledge.

I look at lawyer friends of mine and reflect on the fact that they are called '*learned*' counsel. *Learned, not just experienced.* Learned is what we all need to be. And you don't get to be learned by simply doing your job. You have to put in a lot more than that.

Whenever I watch an orchestra I marvel at the player's craftsmanship (not their artistry, their craftsmanship). These are all masters and mistresses of their job. Out in front is an expert – the conductor. Someone who can visualize in his or her head how *they* want it to sound and *how* to make it sound like that. Recently I saw the Royal Philharmonic perform the Janáček *Glagolitic Mass* at the Brighton Festival, Thierry Fischer conducting. A piece new to me. Astounding. A tour de force. A thing of crescendos, power, passion, virtuosity but above all supreme competence. *These people all knew exactly what they were doing and when they had to do it.*

True success is about acquiring and then leveraging unique expertise. It is not about being ordinary. *The determination to excel is key to success.* If you are determined enough it's mind-boggling what you can achieve. So choose your field, your specialist subject, your niche, and focus on being the very best at it. Everyone is good at something. The tragedy in life is not discovering what it is.

And ask yourself these questions:

☆ What do you need?

☆ What do you have already?

☆ What special talents can you develop?

☆ What weaknesses have you got to manage?

And then it's practise, practise, practise.

3. Think of your career like golf (even if you can't stand the game)

Don't let the analogy fill you with despair. There's one thing common to every golf course. A scorecard. I once helped do the advertising for a huge company called Panasonic. Terry Nagaii was MD of the B2B division and an avid golfer. I asked him if he'd played certain courses – Wentworth, Sunningdale, Walton Heath, Camberley. He had. He summarized his view of each: 'Bad, very good, OK, very bad.'

Mystified, I asked why.

'84, 78, 80, 88,' he replied. Unlike we western romantics who get dewy-eyed about the despicably difficult and horrid Wentworth, Terry's view of each course was entirely coloured by how he scored at each. He had a point.

So why not ensure you keep an honest score of everything you do? After a while it becomes second nature to assess your performance. Because unless you do, you aren't trying to do the one thing that all masters of their craft are constantly trying to do –

Improve

Spend a small part of every week – say, half an hour – working out

☆ what went well;

☆ what went badly;

☆ what *you* could have done better;

☆ how the next week will improve.

You may bore your colleagues by constantly demanding post-mortems, but unless you have them you'll carry on making the same mistakes and you won't improve.

And to conclude, there's one piece of very good news. We can all of us improve even if perfection is denied us. But by practice and setting targets for *everything* you do, you and your team can exceed your own and others' expectations.

These three simple medicines will all help make you more successful:

☆ Enjoy it

☆ Practise improving

☆ Set targets

Importantly, they help you work out if the job is going right. It's unlikely (incidentally) that you'll much *enjoy* what you're doing if you aren't very good at it or keep missing your targets, so this medicine is the most important of all.

Set yourself targets and practise hitting them until doing so becomes the norm.

4 Twenty Signs Pointing towards Success

When you are doing things well there are give-away signs that you are on a 'roll'. Talk to anyone about to be promoted and they say it's like the bionic feeling of falling in love. That out of body. That scary.

'The most successful businessman is the man who holds on to the old just as long as it is good and grabs the new just as soon as it is better.'

Robert P. Vanderpool

HOW SUCCESS FEELS

You'll know when you're a success, won't you? It'll be sort of obvious. The huge office, the entourage of PAs, the Mercedes, the Swiss bank account, everyone agreeing with what you say the whole time, obsequiousness, applause.

No. Sorry. It isn't like that (thank heavens). Maybe once. Maybe in films. Mike Newell said of directing,

> *'Directing is like having a prolonged tantrum. The basic job of a director is to get his own way.'*

And Abraham Polonsky said,

> *'Because we can't be Stalin we become movie directors.'*

In the real world we have to persuade others to our point of view. We have to create and motivate teams. Once when I was being castigated by some of the people at FCO, the advertising agency, for being a lousy delegator, they imitated people playing as one-man bands. Shame on me. I was supposed to be a conductor and all I wanted to do was micromanage and make a lot of noise.

When it first happens, that smell of success, the realization that you are on top of your job, making a difference, a phone call away from an ingratiating headhunter – 'There's a big job at Wondercrunch and I wonder (ha, ha) if you know anyone, anyone at all, who might be right for this job ..?' – a series of symptoms appear. If you feel none of these then maybe success, as most people would know it, has yet to invade your particular space, but I know if you try these out then spectacular success won't be far behind.

1. You are restless

The whole time. You want to move things around and change them. You are a bit irritable because frankly the way things are doesn't seem good enough. Read Tom Peters's *Re-imagine* to see this expressed with real vigour:

> *'Don't … ever … promote 'unangry' people into leadership positions. In fact, don't hire unangry people in the first place. The ideal job candidate walks in, looks you in the eye and says, 'I can't believe this place is so screwed up. But I'm willing to take a chance – as long as I think I've got a decent shot at changing it.'*

Most of us would run a mile from this scumbag of an interviewee but we get the point.

2. You feel like you've only just started learning

You are heavily into asking 'why?' You are a disciple of the Toyota 'Five Whys' – anything that can withstand 'why' being asked of it five times in succession must be OK. For perhaps the first time in your life and certainly the first time in this particular job you are questioning everything and taking absolutely nothing for granted. You've started noticing the most notable bulls***ters in your organization are getting just a little wary of you. You are learning to learn.

3.   And every day you learn something new

Try it. On your drive home ponder the new things you've learned that day. When you get home write them down. Do it every day. If there's a day you've learned nothing, you've been asleep. But I bet you find (being on the verge of success) that you have become a powerful learning machine.

4.   Doing more than you have to is what you do through choice

Your appetite for work has grown. You are greedy for more. You've become a volunteer. You are finding stuff that used to bore you interests you. You are getting involved in things that are not precisely in your area of responsibility. You are helping your colleagues.

I like the late Mark McCormack's mantra:

> 'Don't punch in at nine and out at five if everyone else is putting in twelve-hour days. If you must be a nonconformist why not start by out-performing everyone else?'

People do twelve-hour days to show off or because there's too much to do. This will not please all of you, but working hard is normal today and for most successes sixty-hour weeks are about par. You have to be very brilliant to get away with less in most businesses.

5.   You are showing off less

That axiom of Bob Goizueta ex-CEO and superstar of Coca-Cola is key: 'There's no limit to what a man can achieve as long as he doesn't care who gets the credit.' (US President Harry S. Truman said something similar.)

So stop trying to take the credit. Park your ego. Put yourself second or third. Put the company first and your team second. Interestingly, you'll find you get more successful the less you try to *own* the success of any given project.

Real successes cut the word 'I' from their vocabulary.

6.   You are spending more time at the 'battlefront'

You are beginning to realize you need to feel, see, smell the realities of your market, the outlets in which your products are sold, even the sorts of homes in which your consumers live. *It's about getting real.* It's definitely about getting out of an ivory tower.

Years ago we presented to the Sky Television board when I was at FCO – a bizarre experience in Wapping with the next day's *Sun* being made up in one corner and a squad of investment bankers waiting impatiently to see Rupert Murdoch. He, Andrew Neill and the rest of them were, first of all, impeccably well mannered and good humoured. Despite the crowd outside they seemed to have time to listen and learn.

Rupert Murdoch himself was a revelation as the team talked about the media plan. Nick Horswell, who went on to found PHD, was a bit flummoxed by the level of detail he wanted to go into on posters, a subject of which he apparently knew little:

> *'What sort of glue do they use? Where do they start laying them down? How big is a single sheet in a 48-sheet poster? Why? Is that the optimum size for handling and for cost purposes? How long does it take to train a poster sticker? How many does he stick an hour? When does he do it? Has the technology changed? How could it change?'*

It's out there at the front where battles are won or lost. Life is about detail, not grand plans.

7.   You are obsessive about detail

We live in a world where micromanagement is frowned on. Back to delegators and one-man bands. Yet the best and most powerful CEOs are masters of detail. Jack Welch, Fred Goodwin, Rupert Murdoch and Jeff Immelt, the current CEO of GE. No reason to suppose he'd want to be anything other than his own man – certainly not Jack's man – yet he says:

> *'Stay disciplined and detailed. Good leaders are never afraid to intervene personally on things that are important. Michael Dell can tell you how many computers were shipped from Singapore yesterday.'* (Fast Company, April 2004)

When you start being a success it's funny how good your memory gets and how focused you are on detail. You are responsible, after all, so don't hope 'it'll be all right on the night'. Leave nothing to chance. To ignore detail is to create the potential for disaster.

8. Wood and trees

You are exceedingly interested by the trees, by their leaves, their bark, their root systems. You are an anorak of an arboreologist. But, a bit like that moment when you 'get' maths or see a pattern in a group of works, you can also see the wood. (This is when your anterior superior temporal gyrus starts working, which is called the 'E' spot in your brain – 'E' stands for 'eureka'). You can assimilate and synthesize. You can simplify things so you can see a bigger picture. The moment you do this is the true mark of someone succeeding. Left and right sides of the brain are in accord.

9. You feel good about things

There's a French expression about 'feeling good in your skin'. Of President Reagan it was said, 'he felt comfortable in his shoes'. When you are a success, when you are being successful, however trying the work you are doing, you feel at one with it. Watch any craftsman at work and they make it look easy. Being successful is, in the end, not about hoping for the best. It is about being a craftsman.

10. The laughter is louder, the sensation heightened

Success makes you feel exhilarated. Henry Kissinger said, 'Power is an aphrodisiac', which may be true – Bill Clinton seemed to find it so – but there is no doubt that successful people seem somehow more alive and more aware. More alive, perhaps, because success is fun. Turned on and tuned in.

11. You see good in people: find fault with things

No, success doesn't suddenly make you a paragon of virtue, a touchy, feely, 'let's group hug' leader of people. Something rather odd begins to happen, though. You become a realist about human nature because, if you are to become a leader – one of the true measures of success – you must realize what people can and cannot do. Successful teams play to strengths. They don't moan about their weaknesses. As you begin to succeed you work harder at helping others and coaching them. Jeff Immelt of GE again:

> 'Today it's employment at will. Nobody's here who doesn't want to be here. So it's critical to understand people, to always be fair, and to want the best in them. And when it doesn't work they need to know it isn't personal.'

That last sentence is a bit menacing, Jeff. Very Godfather. But the overall sentiment is fine.

12. Life is a cabaret, old son

You suddenly find you are on stage the whole time. What's actually happening is you are using that most underused organ properly. As Woody Allen said in *Sleeper*, 'My brain? It's my second favourite organ.'

You are questioning everything, challenging everything, pushing back the whole time. You are a bit tiring – some will say tiresome. You are performing 24/7. And you love it.

13. You know what you think

Does this sound so strange? Most people are in the 'maybe mode' most of the time, as this exchange between a rather stupid client looking at a research printout and a researcher shows:

Client: 'What's DK mean, Kevin?'

Researcher: 'Don't know, Derek'

Client: 'Why not, Kevin?'

I leave the rest of that altercation to you.

Knowing what you think and where you stand is second nature to successful people who simply get fed up with saying 'I don't know' or 'I'm not sure' to questions like:

'Do you believe in God?'

'Do you believe in abortion?'

'Do you believe in nuclear energy?'

'Do you believe in the euro?'

'Do you believe in yourself?'

'Do you believe in miracles?'

Spending some time working out your belief system is the mark of anyone who hopes to succeed. Curiously, this is an area where most politicians get low marks.

14. You begin to love presenting

Beware. It's addictive. Like telling jokes. So just make sure you spend as much time thinking about the audience as you do thinking about your presentation. But as you grow more successful your nerves begin to go and your appetite for the stage grows. What's more, with the words of the *Financial Times* thundering in your ears, you recognize it's important: 'Bad presentation is tantamount to fraud.' And you're right.

Scarcely anyone is going to make it near the top of any organization if they aren't a pretty good presenter, be they schoolteacher, vicar, politician or executive.

The CEO of Rentokil performed badly at an analyst's show recently, and when criticized said indignantly: 'I'm not paid to be an actor.'

It's not acting sunshine, it's good manners to be at your best – like dressing decently or using deodorant: 'I'm not paid to smell nice …'

A few weeks later he was fired.

Q.E.D.

15. You spend a lot of time on the move

You are burning calories. You are running around a lot – well, you seem to be in demand and what we call 'over-diaried'. Happens to all sucessful people. You are eating, drinking and talking on the move. You don't need a chair.

But you do need leader reins so those trying to keep up with you can keep you in check. Being successful always means covering ground fast. No, you won't get fat. You may get weary. And you will certainly exhaust those around you: 'Where's he gone now?'

Leader reins, leader reins …

16. You are a laugher and a toucher and an eye contactor

No, you haven't become an evangelist. (Well, not exactly.)

You'll discover most successes are sociable and laugh a lot.

Most people seem to have read Dr Spencer Johnson's *One-minute Manager*. One-minute managers touch people between the shoulder and the lower arm *a lot* – to encourage, praise or even cajole. (I have to confess the cheery doctor scares me witless with his advice, but they say it works. Trust him.)

And eye contact. Well, sincerely folks … and just why are you staring at me in that hypnotic, unblinking way?

These are just techniques and such obsession with style has always irritated me more than somewhat. Most of this 'stuff' works up to a point and for some people, but also try this – *be yourself, be true to what feels right for you, be interested, really interested, in other people (don't put it on). And don't take yourself too seriously.*

That's all.

17. You get more and more phone calls

Successful people are always on the phone. It may irritate us seeing them hanging on their mobiles but the more calls you get a day (not boyfriends, girlfriends, mothers or wives) the more successful you are likely to be. You are quite simply on lots of people's radar.

And if you aren't getting more calls, start to worry. And for your part give 'good phone' to as many contacts as you can cram in. Best example of this that I know is a lovely and very successful guy called Ian George who is MD of Pathé Distribution UK. He is simply the best in the business – when you talk to him on the phone it's telephonic sunshine.

18. You are getting up earlier

Something strange is happening to your patterns of sleep. They say Margaret Thatcher only needed four hours' sleep. You used to scoff at this but now you are waking earlier and earlier.

You've taken to singing at five in the morning.

You're in grave danger of being murdered by those around you.

Your body is telling you something.

'I want to go to work.'

19. But something has to give ...

Success can turn to failure if you overdo it. There was a senior executive who fainted and fell over at a press conference. They said with a nudge and a wink he was 'tired and emotional'. But he was in fact exhausted. His reputation never really recovered.

Get your sleep in.

If you really are a success you probably slept nine hours uninterrupted last weekend. If you want to succeed you'll be booking up plenty of holidays. Mike Kirsch of Norwich Union books his a year ahead. They are set in stone. And you'll be courageous enough to leave your mobile and laptop behind (I know, I know ...). And if you're really brave you'll take three weeks, like the late David Ogilvy, founder of the Ogilvy advertising empire – three weeks and a suitcase of books to read.

You'll also be reading or have read *The Rhythms of Life* by Russell Foster and Leon Kreitzman, which tells you how to use your time to best effect. It will tell you not to do arithmetic between 4 a.m. and 6 a.m., when you'll do it as though you were drunk. It will explain the effects of sleep deprivation. It will explain you are either a morning or an evening person and that not even you, Superman, is both. Success is ephemeral. But there's no need to waste the few moments you have of it by running your engine without oil.

20 But the real feel of success is in the way people listen to you when you speak. That's when you know you've made it.

5 The How-to-Succeed Checklist

'If "a" means success in life then

$$a = x + y + z$$

where work is x, y is play and z is keeping your mouth shut.'

Albert Einstein

MAKING THE MOST OF WHAT YOU'VE GOT

Who was it who said 'If you've got it, flaunt it'?

A part of me (not my brain) desperately wanted it to be Marilyn Monroe. The mind boggles as to what the word 'flaunt' really means. For instance, how would you act out 'flaunt' in charades? And what could 'it' be? Small word for a potentially big subject. But it wasn't a woman. It was Mel Brooks in the film *The Producers* in 1968.

But if you do have the magic, mysterious 'it' you are very lucky and already successful. And if you don't, what follows may help you.

1. Take a long, hard look at yourself

This is top-to-bottom stuff. In front of a full-length mirror. Brutal honesty. Check for negatives. And for any vestige of 'executive presence'.

Haircut

Complexion

Teeth

Glasses

Shirt/blouse

Sweater

Suit/dress

Weight

Stomach

Shoes

Aftershave/perfume

Honestly, now, 'would you buy a used car from this person?' If the answer is 'no' or 'maybe not', you need a makeover. *So strip naked.* I'm not joking. Completely starkers.

Are you out of condition? Fat, puffy, pasty? Yuk. Time for a change.

Welcome to Detox County. Welcome to a new you.

Here's a menu.

NO TO	YES TO
Alcohol	Water
Nicotine	Exercise
Sugar	Fruit and vegetables
Snacks	Balanced meals

But go and read any book. There are diet experts out there but in the end the message is pretty similar – to lose weight, eat less.

But read Suzi Grant's latest book *48 hours to a Healthier Life.* She'll sort you out.

To improve your body, eliminate poisons and drink lots (say two litres of water a day) and take exercise – critical anyway as you get older, just to improve your circulation.

Sounds dull? Well, dull is not what I'm recommending, nor moderation, as what we are actually seeking is immoderate success. This is not about teetotal town. It is, however, about pushing you to adopt the same stringency of regimen Hollywood actors like Brad Pitt and Julia Roberts put themselves under when they are about to do an important part. It's about doing you – hero or heroine of your own movie – justice. *About helping you be as great as you really are.*

So, it's obviously the end of that favourite song 'Cigarettes and whisky and wild, wild women'(if you are female, for this you can read 'attentive young men'), and the effect they have: 'They drive you crazy they drive you insane'.

Quite simply, restyle yourself. Impose change, change that is so critical to what you want to achieve.

Example: If your hair was short, grow it long, and vice versa. Go to a good hairdresser, a really good one.

Example: Go shopping with someone who likes you and who you think has good taste. Buy some shoes and stylish clothes in crisp, dark colours. They don't have to be expensive but I'd prefer they were on the 'ouch!' side in cost terms. It'll make you take the experience more seriously. If you're not sure, go classic. *Most of all look, as though you care about your appearance.*

Example: Start to spoil yourself.

Silk underwear, cashmere socks, Gucci spectacles, brand names you'd aspire to. Take a long weekend in Milan and go to the amazing factory-direct shops. Why is it even Italian taxi drivers dress better than most Britons?

Anyway, enjoy. The trick of the thing is to try new things and to start literally from scratch. If you've done phase one right you'll be a stone lighter with better skin tone, so this exercise will be easy.

Take another long, hard look at yourself in about ten weeks. The effect, *and it is effect we are going for here*, is likely to make you feel very good.

After all, if you can't look after yourself, why should anyone trust you to look after them and their company?

2. Work on your voice

'Why does this matter?' you mutter inaudibly.

Because maybe you mumble, you squeak, you stutter, you stammer, you speak in a monotone, you gabble, you stumble, you drone … Do any of these sound like you, or are you a thespian who commands the room with resounding articulation? If you're not sure, record yourself talking normally. It's very cruel but a useful exercise. Chances are, with a few days' work a voice coach can do for you what a decent golf pro could do for your short game.

Suzi Grant (her again) is a frequent performer on radio and TV, a seasoned interviewer and presenter (hey Suzi, sorry about that word 'seasoned' – you aren't old at all – slip of a girl, in fact, just very practised). She is also a voice coach. Spend a day with her and you'll be dragged through radio interviews, teleconferences, TV interviews. She treats your voice like a recalcitrant slave, beating it up mercilessly, and like a mistress pampering it with lavish praise. The effect is amazing. Your voice will become a tool not a hindrance. It's something you must polish and hone and exploit.

From that very first word you utter you'll notice a difference to the way you feel and the way people react to you. Work on your voice. You won't regret it.

3. Raise the bar

When John Neill, CEO of Unipart, talks about 'what good is' you realize there is simply no choice but to improve your expectations of yourself and others.

No choice but to aspire to be the best.

Because aspiration leads to improvement and improvement is the first step to success. What too few of us do is honestly review how we stack up. Here are seven killer questions to ask yourself.

1. Have you significantly improved in your performance in the past six months? If so, where and how?

2. Can you write down ten things you've learned in the past two weeks? Do it. Do it now.

3. Has your appetite for success grown (or diminished) in the past six months?

4. Have you got smart enough to record everything you've done in the past six months that hasn't worked out as you'd wished, and tell the lessons you've learned from these experiences?

5. What are the next six major challenges you face? How do you plan to succeed in each?

6. Are you enjoying yourself more or less? How do you score in the 'it's good to get up and out in the morning' stakes?

7. How are you getting on with your colleagues? Are your relations with them improving? Is the business getting better, whether or not you are?

Look at the answers very carefully, then repeat the exercise six months later. You'd better see progress, because others around you will make their own improvements. That's how quick the speed of competitive advance is nowadays. But I do have good news. If you do this – and nothing else – you will improve. That's what systematic self-interrogation achieves.

Life is not a continuum comprising dainty steps. It's become a journey with mountains and chasms ('Master, will there be Orcs?' 'Oh yes, my dear, and man-eating spiders and goblins and trolls. Life, my dear, is a horror story and a roller coaster').

But it's also fun. And if there are chasms remember this Chinese proverb: 'You can't jump a chasm in *two* bounds.'

So enjoy it by trying to play on a bigger stage. Too many of us settle for provincial repertory when we should aiming for Hollywood.

It was Leo Burnett, the founder of the eponymous and successful advertising agency, who said, 'Aim for the stars and at least you won't end up with a handful of dust.'

Chances are you are a whole lot more capable than you thought, and you will never find out unless you get out of your comfort zone. Go for gold. Try it.

4. Practise, practise, practise

You'll remember the story of the old lady asking a New York cop directions, 'How do I get to Carnegie Hall?' and his reply, 'Practise, lady, practise.'

You will also recall golfer Gary Player whimsically noting that the more he practised the luckier he got.

The true successes spend a lot of their time preparing. It was Lord Kitchener (he was the guy in the white whiskers pointing out at you in that First World War poster with the cryptic observation, 'Your country needs you') who said in a more reflective moment 'Time spent on reconnaissance is rarely wasted.'

He was right.

The same applies to practice and preparation. I have never ever heard anyone say, 'Judi Dench was over-rehearsed.'

Yet I've heard countless executives say they didn't want to prepare too much in case they lost their 'natural spontaneity'.

Their natural stupidity, more like.

People who tell you this are certainly stupid and probably lazy to boot. And boot them is what we should do to them.

5. Just get it done

In the unforgivingly busy, busy 24/7 twenty-first century the workload is heart-stoppingly intense. I meet executives who have to deal with hundreds of emails every day and dozens of phone calls and several meetings. They can't keep up and it's getting them down. They feel frightened of disappointing themselves and their peers. They are in a cul-de-sac of 'can't do' and negativism. Many of them really are on the verge of losing their self-confidence.

But they are looking at it from the wrong perspective.

Try thinking of every day as a journey from A to Z, not A to lots of other places first and eventually Z if you are lucky. Keep the ultimate destination of Z in mind the whole time and make sure the detours that everyday work brings doesn't stop you getting there. We call this 'focus'.

As executives our job is to *complete* things, not *finish* them.

Finishing anything takes as long as it takes. It involves a step-by-step process. To finish something is to *perfect* it (i.e. to finish it exactly right). This is art. This is ultimate craftsmanship. This takes ages. This is not generally commercially practical.

Completing things is much more pragmatic – it's about getting things done well enough, fit for purpose, as well as can be done in the circumstances, not necessarily exactly perfectly. And that's because you have a limited amount of time available. You get the task done absolutely as well as you can do but within those time limits. In a busy, busy world you can't achieve perfection, you must achieve what's achievable. And you've got to learn to process stuff fast.

So be a completion machine. In the current world there's no choice. There's so much to deal with you have to be great at coping and not being a compulsive 'do it tomorrow' person.

6. Because there's more important stuff to do

What's on your desk and on your PC is process and operational stuff. It's not going to change the world but, like the washing-up, it needs doing.

What really, really matters is getting out into the marketplace, out into the workplace, letting people see the whites of your eyes while you feel the pulse of what's really going on.

I remember years ago when Aldi first came to the UK asking a brand manager at Heinz if they'd been round one of their stores yet. He replied in rather affronted tones that they were much too busy to do things like that. I was running an advertising agency at the time, so I was quite busy too. But not too busy …

So get out.

Meet. Greet. Listen.

If you aren't spending about 50 per cent of your day face to face with real people, something has gone horribly wrong with your priorities and your prospects of success. It's when you are with your front-line people, your customers and your consumers, that you are most likely to have an idea that connects with cash tills. Most likely to see what's right and what's wrong.

Yet the debate in most companies over stuff like this seems to smack of revolutionary thinking: 'You want me to meet consumers?' 'I have to go round the factory?' 'You actually want me to go round some stores?'

Clear your busy, busy diary. Meet some of your peers and customers. Walk around your marketplace. Start learning what's really going on. Successes get about. They never hide behind PCs.

7. Who is that person?

You don't have to be notorious like Jeffrey Archer to be a success.

But it usually helps if people know you. The average wallflower usually has a career that wilts. So how do you avoid what happens to the Tory MP and front-bench shadow Home Secretary David Davis who sat at the top table at the BAFTA awards, or some such, only for people not versed in the mysteries of Westminster to ask: 'Who *is* that man?'

How do you get known? By having a plan, that's how.

And the plan entails what Michael Dobbs's anti-hero Francis Urquhart called 'putting it about a bit'.

It's quite simply 'your own PR plan'. Quite a lot of CEOs nowadays actually employ their own PR person to ensure they stay in the limelight and get quoted. We don't need to go as far as that. Yet.

So take a clean sheet of paper. Write 1–20 down the left-hand column.

Numbers 1–4 are media. People you know or should know in your trade media or, better still, national media (and if you are lucky were at school or university with) and can gently cultivate over a period of time. Listen to them. Help them. Give them what they most want. Stories, leads, gossip. Do stuff for which there is no immediate or obvious payoff (one day there will be, of course).

Numbers 5–12 are your most important, mind-altering-in-their-opinions people *outside* your business. People who make you feel good and vice versa. People you want to stay in contact with. *Forever.* People you will cultivate. People you can help and who can give you advice when you need it.

Numbers 13–20 are the most important people in your own business – not necessarily your boss or his boss but people whom you genuinely think are going to be important contributors to your business's success over time. They might be junior to you. They could be factory people, money people, sales people, whatever. What they'll have is that 'wow' factor that makes them special.

Twenty people who are going to change your life.

Just twenty.

It won't be easy, but the exercise itself will make you really focus.

8. Action Man (1)

Sorry. That should read 'action person'.

Trust me, this PC thing is not a joke any longer. It's real and it's right. Racism, sexism, ageism, any ism is old-fashioned, stupid and unacceptable. And yes, the world has changed. In the 1920s secretaries really did sit on bosses' knees. Jesse Owen was an uncomfortably different colour. Oswald Mosley, to many, had some interesting things to say.

When bluff old Ron Atkinson was fired by ITV and the *Guardian* for being heard on air in the Middle East describing a Chelsea defender as a 'fucking lazy nigger' the world of PC hit a landmark.

Unlucky Ron? No. He's a grown up – at least, we thought he was. Stupid Ron? No. Worse that that. Wrong-headed, ill-principled Ron. And certainly lazy-minded Ron.

The moment you behave with loutish lack of goodwill to your fellow man you are deservedly executed in the twenty-first century.

So be very clear about what is right and what is wrong.

Treat colleagues of the opposite sex properly. The current rash of court cases involving women executives won't stop. There are some very chauvinistic pigs out there. Expensive liabilities to their employers. Merrill Lynch, for heaven's sake, have had to pay out $100 million to female employees in the past year in the USA in compensation.

So don't make sexual innuendos.

Don't harass.

Don't bully.

Don't tease.

Don't show any kind of prejudice – *ever*.

And if you don't show it but do, in the privacy of your own mind, feel it, then sit down and give yourself a talking to – it's old-fashioned and unlike a prospective success. Work out why you feel that way and lose it.

Don't be a bastard to people around you. Not necessary and liable to be harmful to your prospects of success.

And if you do any of these things you can be sure Action Man will be dismembered and put at the bottom of the toy bin.

It's time to start behaving properly.

9. Action Man (2)

After that commercial break on behalf of the 'Commonsense and Decency in the Modern World' party, we return to one of the keys to success as opposed to guarantees for failure.

It's called getting up off your bottom and going out there and doing *it* (the same 'it' that you flaunt, presumably).

We live in a world that demands proactivity. People who seize a challenge and go and sort it out. People who are infectiously energetic and have the urge to sort things out.

To succeed in the twenty-first century you have to be a doer.

'Make it happen,' exhorts the Royal Bank of Scotland – and looking at their quite astonishing rate of growth, they *have* made it happen.

I lose count of the people who lament their lack of time to make it happen, to think or to lead a balanced life. It's Mary Jo Jacobi, a very senior person at Shell (ex-White House, Lehmans and HSBC). *She is Action Woman.* She's amazing. She says, 'When I hear those 30–40-somethings whingeing and whining about work–life balance I just want to smack 'em.'

As the person who led the rebranding exercise of HSBC – does anyone remember the Midland Bank any longer? – she is perfectly placed to pronounce on the art of getting things done.

What would have taken a normal business years to achieve and would almost certainly have ended up as some kind of schizophrenic fudge (the Hong Kong Midland Shanghai and First Direct Bank Conglomerate) was agreed as HSBC and *forced* through by her in a matter of months. This was totalitarian marketing. It worked. An eloquent tribute to the art of doing what needed to be done. Clear. Simple. Final. Hugo Robson, ex-AMV Amro and now in the Cabinet Office, described Mary Jo's achievement as one of the most stunning in modern-day banking. He knew what she was up against.

Successful people are always good project managers, are always good at getting things done. They face up to issues, outstare them and solve them.

10. Time = money = success

The most successful people always have more time than their colleagues. The most successful batsmen always seem to have more time to play the ball than less successful ones.

The essence of success is to have more time to do more things.

Worth repeating that, because it's so important.

'Have more time. Do more things.'

How?

There are a number of ways, starting with being a better, more practised craftsman. David Abbott, who was the best advertising copywriter in my lifetime, used a prosaic expression to remind us we were in a craft trade: 'Stick to your knitting.'

Give yourself the time to be an expert, a craftsman. Because craftsmen always manage to do great work more consistently and more quickly.

What you really need is TIME PROFIT.

Profit is all about margin. Margins are the small bits around the edge.

So increase your 'spare time margin' by arbitrarily reducing the amount of time you spend on what you do.

Example: Cut all one-hour events in your control down to fifty minutes.

Example: Subtract 20 per cent from every meeting you go to and say, 'I have to leave at X ...' and leave then. But *always* say, ten minutes before you leave, 'I have to leave shortly. Can we summarize the key actions – who has to do what by when? Can I also make sure I've got all the issues we discussed right – summarize them – does that check out with all of you?'

You'll save time.

You'll also increase clarity of purpose.

Example: Once a week (just once) get in really early – well before anyone else – say 6.00 or 6.30 a.m. and if anyone else is in smile, say hello heartily, but *don't* chat. This is your 'clear up your desk and all the outstanding stuff' time. In two hours you'll manage to do a week's work. You'd better – that's all the time you've got.

Do not do this every day – you'll wear yourself out, and the surprise effect on other people won't work. Think about it as creeping up behind your pile of 'got to do's' and mugging them.

Final example: Set yourself a programme of 'acceleration':

☆ Speedreading: if you read slower than two pages a minute you have a problem – superstars can devour upwards of five.

☆ Speedwalking: my wife calls it aerobic, I call it exhausting – but it saves time. Just walk twice as fast as you used to (you'll feel better too).

☆ Speedthinking: you do this by breaking issues into chunks that you can deal with fast. Watch an expert at work – they dissect problems into manageable pieces.

☆ Speedeating: don't do it – it'll give you indigestion and flatulence. And on balance, flatulence is not a magic ingredient to success. On the other hand, leisurely lunches are certainly for wimps or fat boys. An hour is plenty of time.

In fact, 'speedeating' is in vogue. Alan Yau (of Wagamama and Hakkasan fame) has just launched Yauatcha, described as 'London's newest and most fashionable restaurant'. You are only allowed to have your table for ninety minutes. This gives them three covers a night for each table. So if 'speedeating' isn't quite in then 'couch-potato eating' is definitely *out*. You are way too busy for that.

☆ Emails and phone messages: this is such a big subject it gets a whole separate section – it's the single biggest 'what do I do about it?' gripe that modern executives have.

11. Add splashes of colour to all you do

We're primarily talking presentations here.

Why does everything have to be Times Roman 12 point on A4?

Why do presentations have to be boringly bullet–pointed PowerPoint?

Why do all meetings have to be the same?

Now the solution to these easily solved conundra is not to wear a baseball hat and a 'let's do team stuff' T-shirt.

It's not about gimmicks so much as *relevant surprises*.

Here are some simple ideas:

1. Make the agenda look *interesting* (use colour, use thick card).

2. Produce neat, *cryptic* briefing notes – all board meeting papers I see are a disgrace or late, which is even more disgraceful. Martin Conradi, CEO of Showcase, is working currently on doing for board and briefing papers what Dorling Kindersley did for travel books.

3. Make current initiatives *tangible* – brand bottles of water, pencils, rubbers, coffee mugs (whatever should naturally sit on a meeting room table) with the name of the initiative on it.

Corny?

Maybe, but very hard to avoid.

4. Encourage *mobility*. Try half an hour standing up. If you can lay your hands on a hot air balloon basket, borrow it and lean on it for an eight-person meeting. It'll be brief. Standing up meetings are. It'll capture people's imaginations. And if it's summer and hot work outside. You are not prisoners of your office.

5. Use *big boards* instead of slides. Try overheads. Encourage scribbling with marker pens. *Big pens usually make short words.* Ban the PC from most meetings – it's a very introspective tool.

6. Be *counterintuitive* – don't always wear the same. Rollneck top, turtleneck, open-neck shirt, tie, T-shirt if you wish (so long it's a great brand). Don't be predictable. Do be stylish.

7. Always try to *get a team thinking*. A splash of colour is inevitably achieved by an easel and flipchart with lots of, obviously enough, different-coloured marker pens.

8. Hard to do, but start to think more *visually*. Life is about more than graphs, histograms and pie charts. Start perfecting your own version of spidergraphs, market maps, planets and satellites and other graphic ideas.

9. *Use TV* so you can look at DVDs and videos that are relevant – a film of a store, interviews with key people, people who couldn't make the meeting for instance, real film that illustrates a point you want to make, like that speech of George C. Scott's in the film *Patton* to illustrate leadership, or even extracts from a focus group can be enormously colourful.

10. Ditto *radio* or any other form of *media* (pages from magazines or papers). News is by definition about making a splash. Fill tables with stimulating stuff. Encourage people around you to use their eyes and contribute.

12. Are you in touch with what's going on?

If you live in the UK here is some mandatory reading – not all of them every day (no one's that good). Just try to keep up.

- ☆ *The Times*
- ☆ *The Week*
- ☆ *Private Eye*
- ☆ *The Sunday Times* and as many 'Sundays' as you can fillet in a couple of hours – keep a pair of scissors to hand and take out anything that seems vaguely interesting.
- ☆ The *Guardian* (occasionally)
- ☆ The *Sun* (how can you be snooty about it? – it outsells all the others and your consumers like as not read it)
- ☆ The *FT* – good, surprising stuff
- ☆ *Time*
- ☆ *The Economist*
- ☆ *The Director*
- ☆ The *Wall Street Journal* (occasionally)

In addition you will find the following rewarding:

- ☆ Listen to the *Today* programme (Radio 4)
- ☆ Listen to Terry Wogan (Radio 2)
- ☆ Listen to Talk FM
- ☆ Watch *Newsnight, Panorama*, BBC and ITV News
- ☆ Watch Sky News and CNN

☆ Watch all the soaps occasionally and anything that people are talking about like, heaven help us, *Big Brother*.

☆ Try to watch new comedy – you get to see what's on people's creative minds if you do this.

☆ Go to as many shops as you can, especially new ones.

☆ Study Trendwatching.com, Springwise.com, FastTrack, Tom Peters's website, Alert Cantos, Adwatch. Become a student of where the best stuff on the web is – places that surprise and delight you.

☆ Travel.

☆ Go to places you haven't been for a while: Liverpool, Leeds, Newcastle, Birmingham. Buy local newspapers to see what turns them on. They have all been transformed. *Look for and devour change.*

☆ Go abroad. Keep on looking for what different groups of people are thinking about, angry about, happy about.

☆ *Be inquisitive. It's the only fit state for a prospective success.*

☆ Listen to interesting people – hear what's on their minds. Older people are often surprisingly wise and worth listening to, especially if you ask the right questions.

13. Have you learned to perform?

Can you get up there on stage and do your stuff?

If you can't, you'd better learn.

This is the twenty-first century.

The new world demands great communicators who have to stand up to a series of antagonists – shareholders, professional investors, journalists, TV interviewers, competitors, your peers, government bodies, lawyers, accountants, trade bodies and so on and so on.

Being only so-so won't do.

As you start to succeed then your ability to stand on stage and be plausible is critical – *it used to be desirable, now it's critical.*

I'd go so far as to say that any board of directors that appoints a CEO or senior executive who isn't an excellent communicator has taken complete leave of its corporate senses.

We expect all the guys en route to the top, or even those leading departments, to be better than competent – if they aren't they'll cost the company a lot of money if and when there's a crisis.

'Why should I bother?' asks the executive Everest climber who inch by painstaking inch has surmounted the corporate peak. 'I'm a leader, not a comedian.'

To survive you need at least mastery in the following:

Sang froid – can cope in a crisis

Charisma – people listen to you

Conviction – a set of values that are consistent

Mastery – of what's gone on, going on and about to happen

To succeed you need to be able to put things across to diverse audiences brilliantly. Like Ronald Reagan did. Underestimated at the time for his intellect (this guy was smart) he was, however, lauded for his ability to communicate. No, he was never a great actor, but he had worked out how to talk to people.

So think Reagan. Think integrity, simplicity, calm, self-deprecating, focus, gentle and convinced that you are right.

You'll be fine.

Of course, it won't always go right, it won't always be fair, and you (if you succeed in reaching the top) will need to look after a lot of trusting people (shareholders – who are people like your mum and dad – and employees and their relations. For every employee in a company the CEO should also think about the other three or four that they are looking after.)

Performing, the ability to deliver with passionate conviction, communicating well, all go with the modern successful executive's job. So enter stage right and start delivering your part with great confidence and panache.

14. Courage, mon enfant

Or – especially – if you have broken through that glass ceiling – 'courage, cherie' – this may not be easy. We are told there's a lot of stress around, indeed 'we are suffering from a stress epidemic', or so claims Richard Excell, the labour market expert at the TUC and member of the Disability Rights Commission. He's right. And he goes on: 'People are subjected to more intensive supervision than ever before.'

Delegation has been supplanted by bullying. You see it everywhere. In the well-reported Cantor Fitzgerald case it's pretty overt and elsewhere it's more insidious.

It's relatively easy to demoralize those around you by denigrating their input – by groaning barely audibly, rolling your eyes, sighing and so on.

If you haven't read Patrick Lencioni's *Five Dysfunctions of a Team* and the behaviour of Mickey the Decision Tech Marketing Director, read it – you'll see subtle bullying tactics brilliantly observed.

We've all been victims of bullying. Sometimes it's imaginary, of course.

I once had a boss whom I thought hated me, or at any rate didn't rate me. Actually, I doubt if he did (the bastard). But I just wasn't doing very well at my job and his behaviour made me worse. But there was one thing I noticed in retrospect. When he left I suddenly got really good. Not just better, but exceptional. A transformation. Fact was, his malign presence made me feel and made me behave poorly. So, to be a success you need to be surrounded by stimulating and inspiring people. If your boss makes you feel lousy it may be time to move or get him moved.

Success for all of us is about creating winning teams and people who feel capable and confident of themselves and each other. Tomorrow, go on a *bully hunt* – create a 'Banish Bullies Campaign' in your office. Aim to make people feel better and track the improvement in performance by everyone.

15. Be a knowledge warrior

We talked about keeping in touch with what's going on. That's essential, of course, and it's probably true that most leaders fail not because power corrupts but because the trappings of power (chauffeur-driven cars, large offices, an entourage of PAs and executive assistants and a permafrost of senior executives) *exclude* the leaders from their market-place and the real truth their customers would tell them. How can a prime minister really feel empathy with the people when everything about the job increasingly isolates him from them?

Sadly, important people are protected from the very things that made them succeed and as time passes they stop hearing and noticing. Even sadder, very few have tellers of truth around them.

But that's only part of the issue and should be easy to solve, provided you are determined throughout your *successful* working life to touch, feel, smell and observe what's going on around you.

Provided, in short, you retain and constantly feed your sense of curiosity.

As you walk (walk – do really successful people walk? You'd better), yes, as you walk down a high street, through a station or an underground or airport, in a store, wherever, *keep your eyes open* to see what's new, what's changed, what's distinctive (in other words, what makes this experience stand out from others).

Stay curious.

But also become a perpetual learning machine. The person who stops learning has lost the will and the equipment to succeed.

It was John Neill of Unipart who said (and I guess I expected him to say 'what tosh' they all were) that he read lots of management books because usually you found something new or something that provoked you into thinking about a work issue a slightly different way.

But, of course, most of the world embarked on the adventure of success feels itself too busy to read such books.

So here's a challenge for you.

If you don't read at least one current 'it's-being-talked-about' manage-ment book a month you are failing in your mission of feeding your brain. At least one a month.

Define what you mean by 'read' Richard Hall, please.

OK. By 'read' I mean degut the best you can get out of it at the rate of, say, 150 pages an hour and generate 2–3 pages of useful notes from that.

Knowledge warriors slay paper at great speed. They also keep their brains active.

16. 'I used to whistle on my way to work ... not any more'

This has to be the saddest lament I've heard. It makes *Death of a Salesman* sound a jolly night out at the theatre.

It was told to me by Roger Alexander, senior partner of Lewis Silkin & Partners, about a French executive he knew:

> *'Why should this once happy executive feel this way? But this is not just him ... there's an epidemic of disconsolate successes around right now.'*

We'll call these people EWs to stereotype them (we all know a few) 'ex-whistlers'.

From the towers of Canary Wharf to the sprawl of Soho and Covent Garden, success for many has never seemed easier to achieve but tasted less sweet or been less satisfying when achieved.

A lot of people used to earn nearly enough to be comfortable. A few, only a very few, got rich. Now there are thousands. Possible to work a 100-hour week for a decade and retire aged late 30s. *Binge working* I call that, with the same attendant disadvantages of binge drinking which are ... well, I forget.

Was a time when people in advertising got in a bit late, had a meeting or two, had lunch (sorry, that's spelt luuuuuuuunnnnch), got back at 3.30, had a meeting or two, had a drink, had dinner (that's spelt with nine 'i's), got poured into bed. And next day did the same. Was this real? Was this sane? Not sure. Can't remember.

The music of those days was a cacophony of 'what if' ideas, film, intelligent people playing with their minds, corks coming out of bottles, knives clicking on porcelain, laughter, yes, most of all laughter.

It was fun. Of course it was.

But, like national service, its time passed. And to be honest, those of us who loved such lives could barely raise the energy to talk on the way to work after such excesses. Perhaps that's why we whistled. We were the 'whistling generation'.

Today is much more driven by left-brain thinking – by numbers, accountability, by covering-off issues with all the stakeholders, by prudent risk management. Lucy Kellaway, an excellent *FT* journalist who's worth reading, said, 'Spare me the dewy-eyed nonsense about creativity'.

But, Lucy, I can't entirely comply because, while a lot of nonsense has been written about it, creativity is one of the things at which we British are really exceptionally good and prolific. If we spare you that we'd be dull indeed.

This dismissive attitude to creativity may at bottom explain why work is becoming a whistle-free zone. As my friends at Trendwatching.com from Holland (one of the more stimulating trendspotting companies around) would argue – and in this Reinier Evers is not flying one of his 'cool kites' (Reinier uses the word 'cool' more often than I've ever heard it used before) but is telling us a universal truth – 'When you see a really robust trend, be sure there's another trend exactly opposite about to happen.'

So just as the whistling stops for some and many are feeling lachrymose, so a new countervailing wave of upbeat and optimism will sweep in. The latter part of the first decade of the twenty-first century is likely to be more like Jollity than Animal Farm.

So start whistling again. To succeed you need to be a source of optimism and, there's a big bonus, you will just be so much better company for yourself.

17. Think simply

Be a master or mistress of what you do but don't over-intellectualize what it is you do.

The US TV football commentator John Madden puts the concepts of thinking and success very neatly: 'The minute I ever start thinking that I'm successful or thinking about what I do … I'm in big trouble.'

Most successful people I know are very bright, quite modest and haven't let it go to their heads. Most of them desperately want to keep their feet on the ground, hard though this is. They want to keep things simple in a complicated world, which is why the other quote I love is this, from an old *Control Data* advertisement: 'The small business's three worst enemies … Thinking too big … Thinking too small … Thinking too much …'

Certainly it's true that in sport thinking too much can be a big error. Jim Boulton, who wrote *Ball Four* about baseball, was greeted on going out to bat by the pitcher with 'F*** you Shakespeare'. No one likes a smart-arse.

Having just talked about baseball, this is nonetheless a very British fault. John Neill of Unipart suggested that being too clever by half, being clever for its own sake and not applying the cleverness to achieve a simple goal, was what had often made Britain infuriating. That old 'great at inventing: poor at follow-through' problem.

Thinking's good for you. But it's also good to empty your mind. It's good to work without agendas. It's good to chop wood and stop intellectualizing. It's also nice to meditate. That's what baths are for. Places to have 'eurekas' in.

Most of all, stop worrying about 'what if x, y, z happens' . 'What if?' can often be the most negative words in the English language – avoid them. Live for now. Go with your finely tuned instincts.

The most irritating thing is to be told 'it's very simple' when you know it's very difficult – at least, that's how you find it. But the great thing about simple is, it's repeatable and easy to remember.

18. 'It's not what you do, it's the way that you do it …'

A lot has been written about strategy. Michael Porter waxes lyrical – no, that goes too far. He writes a lot about it. To tumultuous applause.

Strategy is well defined by Lewis Carroll when Alice says, '*If you don't know where you are going it doesn't matter much which direction you take.*'

All successful people think they are good at strategy, and some are. Yet my problem is that there are loads of good strategists around. (McKinsey & Bain are full of them.) And as you may judge by the way I write, I abhor strategy-speak and jargon. I love homespun stuff like the guy who said, 'Don't put all your eggs in one basket. But if you do … *watch that basket.*'

I was intrigued that in Jack Welch's autobiography the word 'strategy' earns just half a page out of 462 pages. Do I think Jack was a strategist? Not really. He was a 'strategy is hustle' artist. Like Fred Goodwin of RBS (sorry, Sir Fred now. *He* made it happen), who says, 'We don't believe in strategy. We prefer strategic options round here.'

Strategy may be one of the most overrated words in the management lexicon.

This will get me expelled from the IOD and derided by my peers. I may even get burnt. That's what they do to heretics.

The Harvard Business School believe that the thing that marks out the Royal Bank of Scotland as a success was its *executional excellence.* That, I guess, is what characterized the success of the NatWest integration.

I'm a fervent believer in the fact that there a lots of good (even great) ideas around – anyone can have a great idea or a great strategy.

But there are hardly any great products, service companies.

Loads of great film scripts. Very few great films.

Lots of great recipes. Very few good restaurants.

Legions of talented people. A handful of leaders.

It's execution and process that rules OK

So the next time anyone tells you (this, by the way, is constantly being told to me) they are not a good completer/finisher, do me a favour and consider punching them, punching them really hard as you cry, 'it's not a bleeding university – *just do it will you?*' – WHACK.

But refrain. Just glare and go and get someone else to do the completing of the task and say, 'I don't want it finished, just completed.'

If you can't complete or execute you don't really deserve to be in employment. True success lies in execution. *True success lies in results.*

Much of this book has an 'up and at 'em' flavour. But the essence of being a great doer isn't about random action: it's absolutely about having a clear plan and then performing it – brilliantly.

Forget rhetoric and fine words, just be an effective project manager. And you know what? You could end up being a great, world-class performer.

19. No man is an island

You do not get to succeed alone. Few of the signals you get tell you this. You get your own appraisal, your own salary review. Business life has focused on individual and not team success.

The reality is different. Individuals may shine and may indeed be the catalyst to team success, but in truth it is teams that do the big stuff that really runs things.

There is a media myth that it is the leader and he or she alone that makes the difference. Sorry to demur, but Sven (and where would we be without him? *The Times* thundered he was a 'managerial donkey', but that's newspaper for you) is only as good as his players.

So let's talk team.

On this mission to succeed in your working life you need to cultivate the following:

☆ The ability to listen. Ensure you do hear what people say and acknowledge it.

☆ Selflessness. Give others credit even, sometimes, when it isn't due.

☆ The skill of helping. Be *the executive first aid centre* for confused or damaged colleagues. You need them functioning properly. And they need you.

☆ A perpetual sense of good humour. Nothing is *ever* that bad. Nothing. Be cheerfulness incarnate – you'll seldom be hated for it.

As, for the sake of argument, you are doing all this at this stage as a quite junior member of the company, others will notice you and say 'natural leader' (ironic aside – this is the sort of thing people do mutter as asides to each other the whole time. I wish.). Your colleagues whom you are helping will begin to help you too. You are beginning, in short, to build the ingredients of a future team.

Treasure these moments. This is about building the foundation of a fun and fruitful career.

6 Cracking the Email Problem

How to keep the twin horrors of email and voice mail under control.

'If you're in control you aren't going fast enough.'

Mario Andretti

WHAT DO I DO ABOUT MY EMAILS?

I'm constantly told by executives that they've come back from holiday to find 500 emails waiting for them and 100 messages on their answering machine. 'It's ghastly,' they wail, 'I'll be days on the computer and the phone sorting this lot out'.

Nonsense.

Back to old Uncle Jack. Jack Welch. 'Determine your own destiny or someone else will.'

You've made the cardinal mistake of letting two pieces of mere machinery determine your destiny. You have lost control. This is <u>no</u> way to be successful.

In the 1960s, 70s and 80s communication was slower. It tended to be crafted. Look at the heyday of Parker pens and personal letters, look at the golden years of advertising – Heineken, Sainsbury's (the early years), Chivas Regal, Club Mediterannée, Benson & Hedges – all of them beautifully machined and thought through. This was highly precision-engineered communication. These were beautifully conceived conversations full of elegance, nuance and intelligence.

Now anyone can put together a PowerPoint presentation (of sorts), their own stationery and emails, even – I shudder – their own 'ads'. The most uncommunicative lump who really only speaks a language called 'bloke' ('Yeah. All right. Lovely. Nice one.') is nowadays an email or text messager supreme. Texts flow from his fingers. Maybe he's a sneaky would-be success like the someone I knew who used to go into her office on Sundays and do a couple of hundred emails. She called it 'electronic arse-covering'. Everyone kept off her back for the first two days of the week because they were so busy dealing with the issues she'd raised – it was all a bit like a corporate sandstorm.

But we only have to look at the problems big companies face when their emails are exposed to public gaze. (Shell, Parmelat – but the same applied to the Government in the Hutton inquiry).

Advice?

Be very, very careful about what you idly send to a peer. What seems funny or inconsequential one day –

> *'You stupid twit, I told you that profit was irrelevant and now you've had a record month – have you gone mad? Bet you cooked the books. Wouldn't put it past you after what you did in Dusseldorf ...'*

– could have lawyers drooling and sharpening their pencils on day two in a case no one expected but which could end nastily for everyone. All executives need coaching in communication, and especially the art of emailing.

Emails are time bombs. Don't be foolish in what you say and how you say it. Be brief. Be pointed. If in doubt, leave it out. If in doubt, talk face to face to the other party. If in doubt ... you aren't in doubt? You should be – look at the world around you right now.

But how do you deal with 500 of the things at one sitting? Well, you don't do either of the following.

1. Wipe the lot

A senior guy in a major company does this regularly, saying 'if it's really urgent they'll call me'.

Not necessarily.

I imagine such behaviour in a court of law would be viewed as a gross dereliction of duty. It's discourteous and lazy. Right principle (deal with them fast). Wrong practice (ostrich and sand strategy).

2. Go through them one by one very carefully

This takes hours. It treats ice cream spillage and fatalities with equal importance, which is clearly daft. Let's scope this issue.

Five hundred emails take, say, an average of 30 seconds each (200 will take, say, 5 seconds each, another 200 take 20 seconds each, 50 take 60 seconds and another 50 take, say, 2 minutes each). So in theory it'll take you four hours to do this – best do it first thing, say 6.30–10.30 non-stop.

Start by identifying the top fifty and deal with those. Keep your comments brief.

Keep your watch on your desk. You only have four hours, not six or seven. This is like an exam. Imagine the invigilator's merry cry, 'Finish writing in two minutes … put down your pens now and stop writing!'

Oh, just a few minutes more – no, matey, you don't get it. This is a game of brutal clock-watching.

And if you can do five hundred in four hours you can learn to do them in two hours. It's all about concentration, discipline and focus on the realities of business. These are the key questions:

☆ Can you do anything about this one?

☆ Does it need anyone else to be alerted?

☆ Is it for info or an action email?

☆ Is it a code red, code amber or code green email (in descending order of importance)?

☆ Does it smell of a hidden time bomb?

☆ Do you understand

  – what it says?

  – why it's been sent?

☆ What do you want to communicate by your reply:

  – a pat?

  – a smack?

  – a question?

  – a thank you?

  – an acknowledgement?

  – a social response?

  – a lightning response ('crikey!')?

  – a serious ('this matters') response?

  – and so on.

That's about it. Just learn to do it fast and effectively. Your email tone of voice should be as distinctive as your speaking voice, but much more cryptic.

And one more time. If in doubt leave it out. Emails are a tool to be used. Never let them subjugate you.

As regards phone messages, there's a very simple technique. Listen to them all.

Note on a pad who you must call back – presumably most but not all. Better to score points for courtesy.

Call them from a mobile phone wherever it's good and noisy. I favour the concourse of Victoria Station. This means you can be nice and short. I reckon thirty seconds is ages, especially if you've decided before you call what *you* want to achieve.

But try to avoid important as opposed to 'how are you?' catching-up calls on a train or in a car. The former is insecure. The latter is dangerous. Research shows you have the brainpower of someone quite drunk when driving and trying to conduct an important phone conversation at the same time.

Now for timing.

Do as much as you can very early in the morning after a decent night's sleep.

I reckon, however, that 7 a.m. is when most if us are shortest, sharpest and calmest. I know this sounds sadistic but it's also a great time to call. It says:

1. I am awake and on the go.

2. This is important.

If you're lucky you'll speak to an answering machine – so there's even more time you've saved. (If you are an evening person, do it at midnight – more or less the same effect.)

Don't be cavalier with the stuff people send you . If you really do have aspirations to be a leader, take it and them seriously. Be prompt, thorough, well mannered, to the point and brief.

7 The Ninety-day Window

That's about how long you have to prove yourself in a new job – here's how to impress and achieve results.

'Work like you don't need the money,

love like you've never been hurt,

dance like nobody's watching.'

Mark Twain

EVERYTHING HAPPENS FAST TODAY

In other words go for it.

They say the average CEO is allowed a hundred days to make his emphatic mark. I actually think it's less, three months or around ninety days, assuming the poor person works weekends too. My target is safer. It gives ten days' grace which, believe me, you'll really need.

But it's not just CEOs – it's *anyone* doing *any* new job. If about three months into a new post you are still fumbling and feeling your way, chances are before long they'll be leading, you, this myopic performer, to the door.

Does this sound unduly ruthless? Does it sound unfair?

Suppose you employed a gardener and after ninety days he was still wandering around, planning strategy, and hadn't actually mowed the grass. Well, I think you'd have reasonable cause to be disappointed. Suppose you employed a salesman and after three months he still hadn't sold anything ('still getting to grips with the product portfolio and identifying the USP') you'd be telling him USP meant 'useless sales person'.

Everything needs to happen *fast* today. It's what's expected and needed. So the requirements of anyone going into a new job are exacting and pressured. Just don't get there on day one and look gormless. *You've got to land running.*

The following suggestions are indicative of the sort of plan you need. Just don't expect to do a stunning job if you haven't got your 'Ninety-day Checklist' filled in and ready to implement.

When anyone asks you how it's all going (and they will – constantly) just say '*fast*'. Fast never fails to impress in our Formula One culture. And if by asides like this I may seem to be denigrating this culture, believe me I'm really not. Shareholders and employers have every right to expect they employed someone special who was going to bring quick and lasting success to their business. In the process through which you are desperately trying to settle on your killer strategy, remember what the *Harvard Business Review* described years ago – it's my first tip.

1. Strategy is hustle

Not alone it isn't, and there are those who would argue anyway that hustle is a tactic, not a strategy. Ignore them. Set about the first few days of your job with an activity level that staggers, exhausts, appals, motivates (the few around you who are real stars will be excited) and overall impresses all around you.

Fast, then, but not so fast you fall over.

That would *not* be too impressive.

But fast.

Let's face it, you have adrenalin on your side and adrenalin is a potent drug. It can make you do astounding things, like the father who single-handedly lifted a truck off his baby daughter.

Fill the diary.

Demand the *nearly* unreasonable.

2. Why do we all love Dunkirk?

From Harold Wilson onwards that 'Dunkirk spirit' has seldom been far from leaders' lips. It's what characterizes the British. Chaos. Retreat. Water. Misery. Defeat. Sangfroid (that's British?).

No. I'm being totally cynical. *We are all (British and everyone alike) special in a crisis.* We respond with a spirit and a pace of urgency that we should never do in an 'everything is normal' situation.

Look at Alan Leighton at Royal Mail – crisis creator and through crisis aiming to bond the disparate factions together. And it's working, we gather.

So in your first ninety days in your business you *do* have a crisis. A really serious one.

It's about your future.

So articulate the crisis.

Tell everyone how awful and how urgent it is. Describe the state of your business as competitively dire. And set out to solve it.

You will, of course, be helped enormously by the Dunkirk spirit of your colleagues.

And by being new ...

3. A fresh pair of eyes

That's what you have.

For about ninety days.

Thereafter you are a pretty well-established executive.

So be fresh.

And use your eyes.

Don't sit in front of the PC.

Get out, meet people, listen to them and draw some early conclusions.

You are seeing things much as a consumer or a child would. And as a child, don't take 'because it is' as a satisfactory answer. Keep on asking '*Why?*'

'Why do we do it like this? Have you ever thought of doing it a different way? Why not? Why aren't we selling more? Why haven't our plans for selling more been more successful? Why are our competitors as successful as they are? Why isn't our product better?'

Do it with good humour or you'll drive everyone completely mad. And keep the questions relevant to the level of job you are doing. And remember it's 'we' not 'you' – you are part of the team now.

If you aren't a CEO don't behave like one

Keep a record of all you see and all you hear. And force yourself to say to yourself

– What I see is …

– What this means is …

– And these changes must happen because of …

– And in the following way …

– Involving the following people …

Force yourself

It's so easy to sit on the fence. And it's almost certainly not why they hired you.

Use your eyes.

And use your brain.

Remember, you'll notice stuff almost everyone else will tend to take for granted.

4. Out and about

Which is what you must be.

Make sure you get to meet everyone in the business. Look them squarely in the eye, be pleasant, ask them what they do, what they think needs changing and *listen to them.*

Your agenda is twofold:

i) To listen and learn;

ii) To take the pulse of the business. How do people feel about life and about here? Do they even *feel* at all or have they become anaesthetized by boredom or frustration? Are they energetic or torpid? Do you sense they could become lively and effective and fun? Who are the 'good guys'? Who are the problem children? Is there a general sense of their pointing in the right direction? Do people *talk* to each other? Is there a sense of political discord (don't ask if there are politics – of course there are)? *Do you like them?* This last question is quite important. You will have to spend a lot of time with them.

And the way in which you'll do this is by becoming a 'meeting machine'.

Don't just succumb to temptation and do what many people do: retreat into themselves, hide behind their PCs, pretend thinking in isolation beats chewing the fat with their colleagues.

Get out and talk to people: you'll learn a lot.

Mix up 'one to ones' with proper meetings. Make judgements about individuals and teams. See if there is a group dynamic: listen to what people are *really* saying. Most of all, enjoy it.

People are at worst interesting, and at best fun. And remember that they, and how they work together and with you, will really determine your success or otherwise. Whatever you do, look at them as your allies and not as your adversaries. The way people work together is the main reason for a company doing well or not, so make sure you understand them and how to help them work better together.

5. Keep a proper diary

You'll have a good memory.

Surprisingly, most of us do if we are interested in what we are doing. It's only boredom that makes us forgetful in the normal course of events.

But in the first ninety days you have an awful lot to take in and you'll have the insights that only fresh eyes have, and one day these may be really valuable. So write down cryptic notes about everyone you meet, what they say plus your own first impressions and insights. Some of it may be off the wall and provocative but potentially valuable.

My advice, however, is not to do what many do and keep your notes in one big book that may get lost or, worse, purloined. Use a separate pad each morning and afternoon. Staple together the results, date mark them very clearly and leave the results at home. Review the results every weekend and summarize the 'ten insights of the week'.

I also advise you to take down comments in your meetings with colleagues as near verbatim as you can. It's impressive and uncanny to be told weeks later, 'You said – well, your words were pretty well exactly these …' It shows that you, the listener, care about what they say. It also makes any insights that follow less intimidating and more apparently the product of everyone's, not just your own, thinking.

Keep these doodles of yours out of sight. They are your personal, private reflections on a three-month journey.

On average, most of us would expect to have filled nearly a thousand pages of A4 by then.

Lock them away.

You're unlikely to need them again but maybe – who knows? – you'll retrieve them from where you've locked them away one day and find something that someone said that is really important. Have you noticed how lawyers always keep all their old notes? Lawyers aren't stupid.

And if you feel you can't sit through every meeting or lunch scribbling away then don't. You'll remember what was said if you concentrate. Just give yourself ten clear minutes afterwards when you are alone to write out the key points that you recall.

6. Spend lots of time with your boss

Don't live in his or her pocket but make sure you have enough time booked out in their diary so you can review their own expectations of you and their insights of the business.

Recently I spoke to a newly appointed director of a business who had met her boss only once or twice in the initial ninety days and had to book her next meeting a full month ahead. Now her boss was busy, involved in a major piece of extramural work of huge, national importance, but this was clearly ridiculous (and unfair).

So it's not so much lots of meetings as lots of conversations little and often.

Get to know the person.

Get to see them first thing in the morning and last thing in the day.

Get the flavour of them in good and bad moods.

Get behind the facade.

You are, hopefully, going to spend a lot of time with them in the future so you'd better understand them and what drives them.

You don't have to be friends.

You do have to be colleagues, and knowing what he or she thinks and knows (and sometimes even more importantly, what they don't know) will be critical to what you can and can't do and how they will be judging you.

7. Milk that honeymoon

The first few months are wonderful in the sense people are pleased to have you on board – you bring new ideas, new hope, new energy and that fresh pair of eyes.

Don't screw up.

Don't make silly mistakes.

Be sure you are:

– courteous (e.g. that you thank people for their time)

– punctual

– attentive

– reliable (e.g. do whatever it is you say you'll do)

- equable – avoid argument.

- positive – watch your body language (avoid crossed arms and cross looks).

In general, people will be glad to see you. Some will be intrigued, keen to see if you live up to your reputation. Be available to them. Treat them as though they and what they have to say are important. But don't spend too much time with anyone. These are not social events. There's lots of work to get done and 'fast' is the only speed at which to operate. During the honeymoon people will be generous in their expectations of you. Make sure they feel good to have met you. You will need their good will later on.

8. First impressions count

They say we decide whether to employ or not employ a potential candidate at an interview in the first thirty seconds …

If this is true, it's a shame we have to go through the charade of the next thirty minutes. Maybe we should just say, 'Thank you. Next …' after their half-minute is up, like they did in *Chorus Line*.

Whichever way, our own need is to make an impact fast.

Do the following six things:

- good firm handshake

- look people in the eyes

- smile

- listen intently

- talk about the good things you've seen (and the not so good) briefly, clearly, cheerfully and authoritatively

- yes … be *brief* (brief is good, brief recognizes you are on a short, sharp learning curve).

And make sure you really do *enjoy* meeting all these new people, really do *want* to hear what they have to say. This is *not* about acting – it's about doing your job properly.

If you don't and are just doing this glad-handing for form's sake, the smarter ones will suss you out. You may *never* recover if they think you are a phoney.

9. Orchestrate a major event

In addition to this workload – 'the meet and greet show and the day job' – you need to dramatize expectations by setting up a major event at the end of the ninety-day period and let them know it's going to happen.

What's it for?

1. To make you look good.

2. To synthesize everything you've done over this 'honeymoon period'.

3. To motivate your direct reports and their direct reports and your peers.

4. To demonstrate that the world with you around in it is going to be different.

5. To create a distinctive sense of energy and momentum.

Mind you, this is all a high-risk strategy. Get it wrong and you won't recover. Get it right and you'll have made yourself a star.

So do you feel lucky, punk?

How you do it will depend on a number of things, not least your own analysis of the risks and the rewards entailed.

A key consideration will be the history of events in the company. If your predecessor or your peers are notable for their presentation skills and for laying on great events, then do yours very differently from theirs.

Making your mark is pretty important. *You can't simply drift from honeymoon to the rest of your career without symbolizing precisely what you stand for.* In your quest for greatness, don't rely on your own wits. Go to an external source of expertise who can tell you how to do it and set the whole thing up. Whatever you do, don't leave it to the last moment. Whatever you do, don't believe that doing nothing is really an option.

10. Set yourself milestones

If you have ninety days, you have thirteen weekly milestones. Set them down clearly – 'I want to achieve … (put down whatever milestone you want to achieve) … by whichever week'. *Become a ruthless target-setter, starting with yourself.* And if you start missing your milestones, well, I'm sorry to say you'll have to work harder or you've got the targets wrong. So when you do set them down make sure they are realistic and are 'must be done's' not 'nice to do's'. It wouldn't hurt, either, if you let it be known that you are a rigorous target-setter as this will (if they're smart) motivate those around you to start targeting themselves. Go on – be a good influence early on, and if you are beginning to worry that I'm implying you should be working a seven-day week during this period you are unfortunately correct.

I am.

You can take the odd afternoon off, but if you are serious about being a success it's going to be a lot of hard work. Having those milestones means at least you have broken the task into bite-sized chunks on which you can focus.

So that's it.

Ninety days of hell or ninety days of thrilling challenge.

How you respond is up to you.

But one thing is sure. If you follow the advice I've given you, you will hugely enhance your chances of being not just a success but of becoming an extraordinary superstar.

You won't just land running – you'll be breaking world records.

8 Duckling to Swan

How we can transform ourselves even if we'd never really thought we could be a 'success'.

'I may not be a first-rate composer but at least I'm a first-rate second-rater.'

Richard Strauss

GOOD NEWS FOR THE FAINT HEARTED

There are some of us to whom the thought of being a huge success appears far-fetched. We simply regard ourselves as the kind of people who get passed over rather than promoted.

This need not matter if we are perfectly happy in the position we find ourselves but if, on the other hand, we occasionally dream of doing ourselves more justice, of achieving something more than we are currently doing, then what follows will help. It's not a panacea but it is a common-sense piece of equipment designed to allow us to make the journey from 'I'm a failure, get me out of here' to 'I'm glad to have got where I belong and I deserve to be here.' And this is not written for those who are capital 'S' success-driven so much as for those who are – 'SD's – self-deprecators.

1. Be patient

What we are talking about is not overnight transformation. It's a series of incremental steps that are designed to do two simple things:

i) improve your own *self-esteem*;

ii) change the way others perceive you *in a positive way*.

Self-esteem is funny stuff. We really are in Homer Simpson country here. Too little of it, and you realize you really are crap. Too much, and you look preposterous. It wouldn't hurt, for a start, to like yourself a bit more than you probably do currently. It wouldn't hurt to *think about how good you really are* (at whatever it is you are good at – come on, everyone's good at something. Everyone. Remember Forest Gump? Inspire yourself).

But if we are talking about transforming ourselves something has to give, something has to change, which means setting yourself some goals.

Keep them realistic and simple. Say, one milestone a month for the next year. Measure your progress against these. But be patient. Rome wasn't built in a day. The universe wasn't created in a week ... hang on, yes it was. Be ambitious, but don't be too unrealistic or you run the risk of unnecessarily disappointing yourself.

2. Decide what you want

This is not easy.

Most people I talk to struggle hugely over this apparently simple request. Say you want too little and you're seen as unambitious, say you want too much and you're seen as too ambitious and a dreamer.

Most of us, like our friend the ostrich, find it all too hard and just try to avoid the issue. So, Mr Ostrich, look for that bucket of sand in which to insert your confused head. Say to yourself, 'Que sera, sera,' which means it's not your problem any more. Leave it all to Kismet.

You know, you really do have to take charge a bit more. So start by doing something that may seem quite strange. Write a letter to someone you know really well.

Yourself.

It starts: 'My dear ... (well, you have decided that you need to like yourself a bit more, haven't you? And if you haven't made that decision yet, make it now) and it ends 'with very best wishes for a successful year'.

In this letter simply say what you think you should aim for and what you should have on your wish list. Think of it (if you will) as a grown-up letter to Santa Claus.

Post it to yourself and when it arrives and you read it you will find it has a quite astonishingly motivating effect.

3. Focus on everything

This is important.

When I say 'everything' I'm not being unreasonable, just practical. If all you worry about is work (busy fool) you'll be dismissed (rightly) by your friends as a sad anorak. Besides which you'll be a very dull boy or girl.

What else do you do? Here's a made-up list of things a Mr or Ms Average might do.

	Now	By year end
Golf	H/C 24	Down to 20
Pilates	Don't do	Go twice a week
Kick boxing	Never thought of	Get a green belt
French	'O' Level	Improve by 50 per cent
Reading	Read five books a year	Increase to ten
Theatre	Go seldom	Go six times a year
Concerts	Go sometimes	Go every two months
Friends	See sometimes	See them, call them *lots*
Relatives	Christmas only	See them twice a year
Hobbies	If you have two	Get four
Work	Do OK	Do brilliantly ... Do more ...
	Average appraisal	Go for a *great* appraisal

It's really very obvious and based on one of life's great contradictions: '*The more you do, the more you can do.*' Out of which comes the assertion that if you want something done you give it to a 'busy man' to do. *Most of us simply do too little.* We are lazy and probably operate at about 20 per cent of our true potential at virtually everything we do.

Critical on any list of 'must do's' is that related to 'friends and relatives' who you really ought to put yourself out for. See them a lot more often. Be better at listening. Be more helpful.

It'll be great for them.

It will make you feel terrific.

Bottom of the list is 'work'. That doesn't mean it is the least important thing, just that it is only *one* of the things you should think about. And, if you will, indulge me in this one very important oxymoron. Write it down and put it in your pocket:

WORK IS FUN

Start thinking it might be fun and you should find it *is* fun.

4. Work harder

Welcome to the apostleship of the Protestant Work Ethic. Welcome to the sweat shop. It's almost un-PC to say '*Work harder*', isn't it? We all work too hard already, don't we? Too many exams. Too many hours. Too much stress.

I actually think we work as a nation rather little. Our productivity is not good. We talk about the sweat and misery that was the consequence of the Industrial Revolution. But there is little of that around now. The revolution ground to a halt. I disapprove of sweat and misery. But I approve of work. Especially smart work.

Especially people who focus on what needs to be done, work out how to do it well and work away at it until it's done. I love positive people whom I constantly meet, and most of these do work incredibly hard.

The list is long but here are some of the unsung heroes and heroines. People brilliant at what they do. All real successes, although if you actually asked them they might not see it that way. You don't have to be John Prescott to be a heavyweight success – you do have to be a player. These guys are players.

Kerrie Barker my hygienist, to Jay who runs the best newsagents in Brighton, to Lisa at Showcase, to Linda at Argyll, to Jullet at Shaftesbury Homes, to Philippa and Amy at Skinnydip, to all the heroes and heroines who have prostrated themselves before the great god of work, arise, you are saints and successes.

Join me and them in a glass of champagne to celebrate that WORK IS FUN.

5. Get rid of that bushel

People hide their lights under bushels, or so the cliché goes. And I'm sitting here wondering why on earth all these people are going around holding their candles, trying desperately to stop them going out and asking passers-by 'Have you seen a bushel, mate?'

What is it? A small bush, a particular kind of bristle, a diabolic form of omnibus, a kind of French scarf, a woman from Shepherd's Bush? (In fact it *was* a wooden or earthenware container.)

Undue modesty doesn't pay.

Say that louder.

UNDUE MODESTY DOESN'T PAY

Most of us hate blowing our own trumpets (especially near bushels – don't these clichés freeze your brain?) and understate how good we are. And because we are modest to others we are criminally modest in *our own* ambitions. When my wife phones my mother-in-law she always says, 'Hi. It's only me.' It drives me crazy. What does she mean, 'only'?

Actually, this is grossly unfair – this isn't about her self-esteem, it's about manners. Were she to say, 'Hi, this is your very important eldest daughter,' I would be surprised and dismayed. In fact, I'd think she'd been reading this book.

In talking to Sir Peter Davis, formerly of Sainsbury's, I was very struck by how focused and clear he was about what he'd done and not done in and in what order. He was very concerned about accuracy. No shrinking violet he, but he didn't come across as bombastically egotistical either. Just clear that if he had done 'x' he was going to say he'd done it. Mike Kirsch of Norwich Union is the same.

So unless we tell those around us

(i)   what we've done,

(ii) what we can do,

(iii) what we want to do,

(iv) what we are doing now,

(v)   what needs doing,

we can't expect them to take us seriously or to know what we are capable of – especially as, chances are, we've been hiding ourselves let alone our lights under bushels for some time.

As the third cliché goes, 'It pays to advertise'. So tell people around you who you are and what you do. And if you haven't got anything to say then find something good. Is that OK as bushel-demolition material? Will you now agree to put your name up in lights?

6.   Hallo, Big Ears

I was always a bit suspicious of this Enid Blyton creation. Heaven alone knows what he and Noddy got up to. At least Noddy had some sort of career as a campanologist and he did enjoy material benefits in the shape of a nice car. As far as I could see Big Ears was just a hanger-on and a sponger with a form of facial deformity it is inappropriate to mention in today's PC world.

Perhaps I'm just being unkind. Apart from his apparent lack of courage he did, however, seem to have a knack of listening. He had to use those ears for something, I suppose. And this is what *you* need to do.

The art of listening is the biggest single key to your succeeding.

Think of your ears as antennae, the centre of your radar system. They tell you what's going on, who's doing what, why they are doing it, what people think of you – and that's important, because if you don't know this how can you actually change their perception of you?

It sounds easy – listening.

It isn't.

If you aren't used to it you've got to practise.

Distinguish between listening (that's keeping your ears open) and hearing (that's receiving things through your ears). It's not just about having big ears, it's about how you use them, too. If you listen it's amazing how much more interesting and well informed people will find you and, indeed, how much better informed you'll be.

7. An amazing source of energy

That's what you need to be.

With almost everyone who is either not very successful or not very well I am used to hearing them complain, 'I just feel so tired.' They are listless, unfocused, demotivated and bored. They are often parodies of couch potatoes, voracious consumers of snacks and junk TV. Not surprisingly, they can see little in life to excite them.

Well-meaning advice like 'for goodness sake pull yourself together' has minimum beneficial effect. It's a bit like shouting at a fire 'cool down'.

This is a disease.

And the malaise manifests itself in zippo energy. The fuel tank is empty. Press the 'let's get on with it' mental accelerator to the floor and nothing happens.

It's also a vicious circle that's very common. The less you have to do the more tired you get. The more tired, the less you can get done.

Changing this into a *positive circle* is as easy – well, relatively so. It involves, literally, filling the fuel tank with a list of things to do, volunteering to do stuff, creating a schedule, getting up really early in the morning, saying constantly 'I'm enjoying this' (amazing how credulous your psyche is), ticking off 'done thats' on your mental 'to do' list, being purposely busy, being constantly cheerful, resisting any vestige of temptation to be introspective (because it's inside yourself that most of the problems lie, usually) and finally consciously increasing the pace at which you do everything – walk, talk, type – everything. Whatever you do, do it faster. Peter Senge, author of *The Fifth Discipline*, describes the American corporate preference when it comes to growth as 'fast, faster, fastest'. The Americans have a point.

Energy is self-perpetuating, and the more energetic you are the more energetic you'll feel. You need to take this in stages, but finding more energy is a bit like running. The more you do the more you can do. The endorphins kick in.

Without energy, seeking any sort of transformational change, let alone success, is not just hard – it's impossible.

8. All together now

OK. There'll be the odd entrepreneurial exception, the exceptional loner, but in general terms it's the teams that win, not individuals. And it's teams that build by their collective approbation the individual self-esteem. In simple terms, 'you can't do this all by yourself'. So don't try.

Years ago, funded by the late maverick politician Bernie Grant, a one-time West Indian test cricketer, Reg Scarlett, set up the London Cricket School in Haringey. Its mission was to take athletic young people, mostly but not exclusively Afro-Caribbean, who were failing at school and in life and give them a new chance. If they worked in the morning at their lessons they got to play cricket in the afternoon. That was the deal.

Some of them had never played before, but under Reg's tutelage and the simple concept of them always practising in twos (Reg said each fed off the improvement and enthusiasm of the other and became socially responsible too) they became good enough to put out teams that beat County Young Professional sides and produced players like Mark Alleyne, Keith Piper and Adrian Rollins.

Reg realized no one could do it either alone or anonymously in large groups, so he created the concept of '*improvement partnerships*'. It's what happens in intense sports like kick boxing, judo, karate (imagine trying to get better at any of those by yourself?). In your mission to succeed you must find others who also want to improve their prospects, and you must work with them. You'll feed on each other's improvements and achievements.

9. Spoil yourself a little

I don't, despite my constant cries 'work harder' and 'improve your energy levels', believe very much in brutal regimens.

The old-fashioned 'more stick, less carrot' school of management has long passed. Most people respond best to having their views listened to, being praised for doing well and coached in how to do better.

Joh Neill of Unipart says he remains appalled at the relative absence of training in the UK although, he says, it is getting better. Better but not good enough. To raise our standards we all need constant sharpening, constant coaching. Even John Neill needs it.

We also need to be good to ourselves.

When did you last reward yourself?

Amazingly, small treats bestowed on yourself (provided the largesse isn't constant and excessive) have a hugely beneficial effect.

Yes, you are allowed to tell yourself, 'well done'.

Yes, you are allowed to celebrate a little.

And yes, you are allowed to do something really important, which is to make, just occasionally, a bit of a fuss of yourself. So long as that fuss doesn't just comprise a lengthy sit down with a box of Milk Tray in front of a DVD. *That's not making a fuss of yourself – it's making a mess of yourself.*

Develop this system of self-reward so you start to say, 'if I manage to do X I'll give myself Y'. Change from the sort of person who used to give themself things as a consolation to someone who gives themself things as a reward. From 'I'll have a drink because I feel fed up' to 'I'll reward myself with a drink because I deserve it'. And for 'drink' in this new, slimline, muscle-toned world read whatever is 'suitable' – say a new book, CD or session in the gym. Doesn't matter as long as *you* regard it as a reward.

10. Honesty is the only policy

Facing the truth is sometimes hard.

This section is addressed to those whose appetite for success has been dormant or whose self-belief has been rocked or simply not developed. And for them to achieve what they can – and truly in nearly every instance I encounter quite amazing improvements – requires a large dose of honesty.

Unless you can self-appraise honestly you can't set yourself achievable milestones nor make those self-rewards have any effect.

As Alice might have said (but didn't), 'If you don't know where you are you can't know where you are going.'

So where are you – *honestly*?

Write down on a sheet of paper what you are good at, what bad at, and where you want to go. Try this as your 'Truth about Myself Checklist'.

(a) I am really good at the following five things … (I want five not three, so *concentrate*).

(b) But I could be much better at … (what? All five, four, maybe just three? You decide your priorities).

(c) I am awful at … (I want four of these, and if the list is longer then just the top four).

(d) I really like doing these things at work … (three will do).

(e) And outside work … (three again will do).

(f) These are the three things I'd like to achieve this year …

(g) In a perfect world with me in shape, my dream job and dream life would be like this … (write it briefly, but write it).

(h) My self-esteem on a scale of 0–10 (where 0 = 'I have none. I'm a turkey' to 10 = 'I am the greatest, everyone bow down before me'). Where do you come – where do you want to come?

Fill this in honestly.

And revisit it every six months and do it again six months later. See if you make progress. I'm willing to bet you will.

The better you get the more honest you can be to yourself and, you'll discover, you become self-critical in a more constructive way than you'd ever expected.

There is no magic bullet to success. If there were, everyone would be a success, which would mean that nobody was, so we'd have to start all over again.

What this is all about is trying to cajole all of us to be true to our own abilities and develop our strengths.

If you don't believe it is better to develop and move forward than stagnate then I'm amazed you're still reading this. But on the basis you're thinking 'I'd like to do better', then try this stuff. Try it, because it'll work and it'll be fun.

To leave you on a positive note, *I'd guess you probably are at least twice or three times as good as you think.* Chances are you could be a quite remarkable success if you tried harder, focused yourself, worked with others and laughed a lot more.

If I'm right, what's stopping you? I've given you some ammunition, so start shooting.

9 Learn to be More Self-confident

No one feels self-confident all the time – no one – but improving your confidence, or at worst, keeping up pretences makes everyone feel better – most of all you.

'Where did we go right?'

Zero Mostel in The Producers

'On the whole human beings want to be good but not too good and not quite all the time.'

George Orwell

WALKING THE WALK

How I hate that particular slice of apple pie … walking the walk and talking the cliché. Not quite as bad as the man who got fired from M & S because of his appalling temper who persisted in telling me: 'When the going gets tough, the tough get going.'

Yet again it is Jack Welch who gets it right when he says:

> *'Legitimate self-confidence is a winner … the courage to be open, to welcome change and new ideas … relish the intellectual combat that enriches ideas.'*

And in all my experience, people who walk into a room with the assurance that all is well and they are glad to be there and eager to learn something new, well, people like this get invited back.

Confident does not mean arrogant, people like this very often do not get invited back. No one likes a smart-arse. Everyone hates people who are cocky. Sadly, we meet a lot of them nowadays on trains braying into their mobile phones. They sound empty of feeling rather than full of confidence, although they do at least seem to know where they are: 'Hallo, mate, I'm on the train ...'

Confidence is about comfort, about being so comfortable with yourself you focus on other people. Arrogance is about overestimating yourself, trying too hard and focusing on yourself.

The advice that follows is designed to help you feel better about yourself. Don't do what an advertising executive I knew did, which was to throw back a slug of neat vodka before a presentation to make himself feel better (or so he claimed). Do it the natural way by becoming more self-aware, working out when and why you feel at your best and trying to repeat that, finding triggers that improve your morale (OK, lots of metaphorical shots of vodka, I suppose) and work on developing your own peace of mind.

1. Be less introspective

Maybe it's pressure of work, maybe it's stress, but an increasing number of people are becoming very inward looking. It's not helped by what Eugene Beer of Kaizo has described as 'irritable desk syndrome', which is what happens to executives trapped behind their PCs. The phenomenon leads to agoraphobia whereby people simply don't want to go out.

So resist that 'I'm too busy to move from my screen' lie.

Get out. Go to stores. Visit customers. Walk high streets. Observe consumers. Read magazines. Listen to radio talk-ins. (That last one sounds like masochism but stick with it: you'll learn a lot, not least the language real people really use, people – you know, 'consumers', the people who pay for the life you lead.)

2. Spend more time 'thinking'

I've heard people say it: 'I really haven't got time to think.'

Oh, really? Surprised you've got time to breathe ... or live, come to that. Busy people. Busy lives. Busy, busy, busy. We live in a 'get it done' (or at any rate an 'appear to be doing it') culture so there's no time to 'wonder why', to be, quite simply, questioning.

We need to spend a few minutes every day thinking – whoever we are, whatever we do. And if you don't know how – after all, there's a fair chance you may be out of practice in the art of thinking, being so busy and all that – well, it entails being still and letting your mind work. Like this.

You take a blank sheet of paper and say to yourself 'I'm going to *think* about three things I did today' (side one) and 'three things I'm going to do tomorrow' (side two). And against each 'thing' write down a note on something (whatever) you think is important – such as

Sales meeting – slides terrible last time – use proper slide producer

   – no chance of getting X onside – pre-meet to explain the issues?

   – implify sales message? Six-second sell ...

Cryptic, simple 'think points'. Give yourself, say, five minutes on each with a view to thinking out a better way and seeing if there's really anything obvious you've forgotten about or something new you've never thought about before.

The process of doodling on a piece of paper and generating the odd thought soon begins to develop into something more exciting. We call this 'creativity'.

There's also something you'll discover from all this thinking, apart from the fact that the more you do the better and more productive you get.

The more you think, the more confident you'll be.

3. And you'll be more inquisitive

You'll carry around the word 'why' like a gardener carries a trowel, constantly using it to dig away and prod things you aren't sure about. Take nothing for granted. Having the balls to ask enough questions to ensure you really do understand what's going on is a good idea.

A very bright young executive said to me, 'We went into this presentation recently without really knowing what our boss or our boss's boss really wanted.'

How can you get anywhere if you don't know what the destination is? Create a regimen in which you say to yourself, 'If I haven't asked "why?" in the last two hours I've lost my touch, my appetite or I've gone to sleep.'

4. Become a listener and a hearer

There will be moments in this book of déjà vu. I apologize for being if not so much repetitive but insistent. This bit is about paying attention. Let's see if you have been.

A lot of people *listen*. Not many *hear* what's really being said.

A lot of people *look*. Not many *see* what's really going on.

If you hear and see and feel the vibrations you'll be enormously self-confident.

Think of the people talking to you and the world around you, not of yourself. This sounds a little obvious and trite. Easy to say, until you are carrying the woes and worries the average executive is carrying. Try telling them to relax. It's not only unfair, it's unreasonable.

I really do understand. But just try smiling, nodding as people talk to you and, yes, really, really listening to what they say. The impact will be electric.

One other thing. Always let people finish their sentences. Don't be the eager smart-arse who butts in and presume he knows what they are going to say – it drives people crazy. I know this. I used to do it. Guilty, your honour.

5. Live in a world of contrasts

The worst state for most people is that flat and tiresome serenity that 'No. It's OK. It's fine. There's nothing wrong' brings. This, by the way, is an advance on the dreaded 'Comfort Zone' – it's the '*Doze Zone*'.

People can be very content in this state until someone challenges them. Give them any of that 'intellectual combat' to which Jack Welch refers and toys are thrown from prams. Self-confidence evaporates. That's why having a very varied work and social life *trains* your mind and body to work at a series of different levels. They used to talk about 'Renaissance Man', now they talk about 'Renaissance Manager'. It goes beyond pluralism. It's about being involved in so much that the engine is running at its most productive tilt. But you are not a piece of factory machinery, so this analogy doesn't really work – you are a finely tuned creative piece of work that needs to work at varying levels to maximize your sense of self-respect with, for instance,

- huge activity

- but periods of great stillness

- long, loud laughter

- and quiet, reflective chuckles or even tears

- frenzy

- and methodical activity.

Try to vary pace, content and intensity.

Observe what happens. Your body is a temple (Oh no. I am so sorry about that. I do apologize. I'll never say that again – I promise). Just avoid the same old, one-paced living. Working at a constantly varied pace will do wonders for the way you feel about yourself.

6. Being a very, very nice man (or woman)

It's that old line from the AA advertisement. And what I'm getting at is the power of smiling and being a nice person. 'Hang on', (you say) 'don't bastards win? Aren't they the ones brimming with self-confidence?'

Wrong script. It's being good-humoured, attentive, polite that gives you power. You get your own way much more often this way. The world of the bastard is over. Ask Merrill Lynch.

Consider two forms of complaint in a restaurant. 'Hey, you bastard, this meal was awful and I'm not paying.' Well, that's a great example of charm school, likely to start a fight and prove damaging to your self-confidence and your nose.

Alternatively, 'Excuse me. I'm afraid something's not quite right with this dish'(said quietly). This, accompanied with a smile, will get a concerned 'how-can-I-help?' audience. No winners. No losers. A conversation. Self-confidence high on both sides. A problem. A solution. Hey, let's face it, they aren't trying to piss you off. You are the customer. It's your meal. And you are their meal ticket.

7. Have the power of your convictions

You have got convictions?

Things you care passionately about. Just a few, perhaps.

You do know exactly what you think, don't you?

For most the answer is 'not really' because you've been too busy to have thought about it – and we've already covered that.

The issue is to *be powerful* in the way you express your views, not to do so in a limp-wristed, apologetic way. Powerful does not mean dogmatic, abrasive or aggresssive. It means vivid. It means descriptive. It means – for heaven's sake – *alive.*

And if you want to be *convincing* – if you ever want to sell anything you'll have to be – make sure you can talk winningly about your convictions. Look, let's make this easy for you. Write down your top ten convictions now – *stuff and things you really believe in.* Now think about each and how to talk passionately about them.

'Passion' is a word over-used in business today only because there's so little of it around. *Be passionate and the self-confidence flows. Be cerebral, stay nervous. Your choice.*

8. Tell the truth

And then you don't have to remember what you've already said – that was Richard French's claimed reason for doing so (he was the founder of FGA and FCO, two of the most creative advertising agencies of the 1970s and 1980s, and was himself one of the most supple thinkers in the communications world). It's a compelling reason.

There's another.

Nearly everyone is a rotten liar. They go red. They shuffle from foot to foot. They stroke their nose (this is apparently a big give-away – Clinton kept on stroking his (his nose) in the Monica Lewinsky hearings).

So why bother?

Only one thing is worse than lying – being found out. And you will be. Then no one will believe you again.

And it's wrong. Time to call a halt on expediency and success at any cost. If the series of corporate disasters of recent years and the contempt with which politicians are generally regarded are going to teach us anything, it's that telling the truth is what people expect nowadays. How about honesty as an entry price? No, please don't laugh, I'm deadly serious.

9. How you look

The occasional politician like Ken Clarke derides the impact of dress sense. He is so bombastically full of self-confidence it wouldn't actually matter if he were to dress in rags. But for most of us it really matters and does make a difference.

There's the old-fashioned school. Michael Gerber says if you wear a sharp blue suit and white shirt with a dark tie that must have some red in it, you'll sell more than if you wear anything else.

What the hell have you got to lose? Try it. See if you sell more.

Then there's the dress-down school. Dress-down Friday at most corporations saw the old C & A sweaters come out. You see, the trouble is the average guy in the UK is hopeless at casual. They just look scruffy. Actually, women and the Italians do it so much better.

The simple way of doing this is to copy the way someone else does it. Look at magazines. Find a role model you admire and do what they do in your own particular way.

It's really important to care about what you wear. It matters because it says something about you. It says you care, apart from anything else.

And the better you dress the better you feel.

10. Confidence is about learning

Every day you learn one or two new things. And you promptly forget that you have.

So every night write down two things you learned that day. Every night. And use what you've learned. Your confidence will increase as you find yourself able to recall interesting meetings and learnings from months back. Be a 'learning machine' and you'll learn to be in command. You'll also learn self-confidence.

The whole issue of self-confidence springs from being comfortable and secure in what you do and are trying to do. Confusion, lack of self-esteem, fear, ill-preparedness all conspire to make people uncertain and apparently lacking in confidence. And this confidence thing matters, it really does.

Because if you aren't confident why should others be confident in what you say? Or in what you make, or do, or recommend?

Perhaps the single most important key to securing success is the confidence with which you attack life. These tips help, but nothing substitutes for being technically good at your job. Great craftsmen not only make it look easy. They look and feel confident too.

For those of you for whom self-confidence is not an issue, following the advice I've given will make you feel even more comfortable and competent. The great thing about life is that everything can get better; you never reach your zenith; the grass truly is greener the other side of the fence. And as the dreadful Annie in the eponymous musical said, or rather warbled, 'The sun'll come out tomorrow.'

10 The Postitive Lessons of Failure

Failure. It's frightening but it's a good thing. Stop looking behind you and start thinking ahead.

'Like one that on a lonesome road
Doth walk in fear and dread,
And having once turned round walks on,
And turns no more his head;
Because he knows, a fearful fiend
Doth close behind him tread'

Samuel Taylor Coleridge, The Rime of the Ancient Mariner

'Greatness is not necessarily found in success but as a response to failure'

Michael Marley, former PM of Jamaica

FAILURE AND WHAT IT TEACHES US

I recall my tutor at Balliol, a nice, urbane man, Dr Roger Lonsdale, saying as his toddler walked determinedly into a door, 'Ah yes. Pain is a great teacher.'

This the man who wrote a long and learned essay around Pope's couplet,

'and thriving plants ignoble broomsticks made
now sweep those alleys they were born to shade'

which, when you think of it, is as eloquent a testimony as you could find anywhere to social change and the decline in fortunes that change can bring to those previously successful.

Yes, pain is a great teacher but so too is failure. In its own way it is so much more instructive than success. Success depends on so many factors all interlinked so that actually building a robust success model is quite tricky. Easy enough for the respective companies to open successful Tesco, Next or M&S branches. They're doing them from a tried and tested prototype. But try to repeat the 'Tesco Success Model' and you'll recognize just how hard it is.

Learn about failure. Be honest about the things that didn't work out the way you thought they'd happen and engineer out the flaws, and hey, you could be looking at a new way of succeeding. My excitement about all this came from a book by Frederick Reichheld called *The Loyalty Effect*. In the heart of his book is a great chapter. It parodies Tom Peters and Robert Waterman's best-selling book *In Search of Excellence*. It's entitled 'In Search of Failure'.

He quotes Warren Buffett, whose success in business and his ability to laugh at himself should appeal to us all. Here's Warren speaking to the Emony Business School in 1991:

> *'Albert Einstein said "invert, always invert in mathematics and physics" and it's a very good idea in business too. Start out with failure and then engineer its removal.'*

The idea that when a system is working well it's very hard to explain just why, is sound. This phenomenon presumably inspired the aphorism 'if it ain't broke, don't fix it', something contemporary gurus in management teaching tend to despise. More fashionable today to say, 'if it ain't broke, break it'.

Buffett argues that it is far more productive to select shares in your portfolio of companies *not* performing at the top of their game. What a little 'failure engineering' can achieve is to make them a lot more valuable, a lot more productive, a lot more successful.

Reichheld speaks only briefly about the universal fixation with success. The fixation with extraordinary achievement is very deep-rooted but we create mechanisms to divert our gaze from the horror of failure. Bureaucracy does that beautifully. As neat a packaging concept as you could imagine, because it creates a whole series of escape hatches into which the things that didn't work can be parked and forgotten.

And when senior executives fail, as nearly all of them eventually do (proof of the mortality of even these masters of the universe), they are despatched much as we used to despatch the Chancellors of England in Tudor times. Bloodily and publicly. It provides great media sport. *Schadenfreude*, the Germans call it.

And there's a whole book devoted to the subject – Sydney Finkelstein's *Why Smart Executives Fail*:

> *'Are major business failures ever really due to stupidity or lack of talent? The reality is that people who become CEOs of large corporations are almost always remarkably intelligent.'*

So that's all right, then.

You are a remarkably intelligent failure, which puts a completely different complexion on all sorts of things – like being, for instance, a good-natured Nazi. In fact, robust a study as it is, Finkelstein's book makes remarkably depressing reading. Its 300-odd pages are proof that we all live in failure denial. There's only so much *Schadenfreude* you can take.

The reality of failure today is that, just as 'anything is possible' (remember that old Saatchi mantra?), so too does the sheer speed of change mean that more businesses and people will fail before (as it were) they've even got their eye in or because they are playing the wrong game. Bill McGowan, who founded MCI, once said,

> *'the chump to champ to chump cycle used to be three generations. Now it's about five years'.*

Another ex-CEO, Paul Allaire of Xerox, said,

> *'we're in a brawl with no rules'.*

So it's rough and tough and the name of the game is something more totalitarian even than *Rollerball*. Maybe failure is inevitable and the old version of great companies surviving through generations (read Jim Collins *Good to Great* to get a handle on this) is over.

'*Memento mori*' they used to tell the most successful Roman generals as they paraded in triumph. Derek Davis, high-flyer at the DTI, told the assembled glitterati at his valedictory drinks do all about this: '*Memento mori* didn't actually mean "Tell your secretary to book a date with the Grim Reaper!" It meant, "Don't get big ideas. You're just an ordinary bloke like the rest of us."'

So how do we ordinary blokes get to be as successful as the bloke in the chariot? Samuel Beckett, hardly a Minister of Mirth, proclaimed:

'*Go on failing. Go on. Only next time try to fail better.*'

Tom Peters (yes, him again) says in agreement that you must

'*Fail faster. Succeed sooner.*'

OK Tom, let's analyze that, shall we? I think you mean 'do more stuff, some of which inevitably fails and, given the law of averages, some of which will succeed'. It's canal boat theory, is it? The more canal boats you put into a canal the further along that canal you'll push the boats in front of you. Or is it what we in the south-east of England call (and this is a technical expression) a load of old bollocks? Have you noticed how the older he gets the louder Mr Charisma Peters shouts and the angrier he gets? No wonder his logo is a big red exclamation mark. He is literally playing the Peter Finch lead in the film *Network* – the newscaster who says on air, 'I'm as mad as hell and I'm not going to put up with it any more.'

More of anger later, because Mr Peters has a point. Success rarely comes from being content with your lot and nearly always comes from getting angry and energetic enough to insist on changing your lot.

The best example of this 'fail to succeed' stuff is the story of Robin Cousins, the British Olympic skater. In his early days when he was winning a lot of competitions he decided, as so many British sportsmen do who become what they call 'world class', he'd have to train in the USA. His American coach watched him skate and to Robin's consternation declared he was no good and unlikely to progress further. Robin asked why. The reply was highly instructive to Robin and to the rest of us: 'You just don't skate to fall.'

So unless you are prepared to risk failure you are unlikely to win success. Playing safe is not an option. No way, screams Uncle Tom Peters: 'Sensible baby steps won't cut it, I'm afraid. No, the CEO challenge today calls for broad leaps … big plans … staggering risks.' If he has his way we'll spend a lot of our time falling, a lot more than actually skating. But hear what he says. That the seeds of success lie in failure. That's the good news. Oxymorons often are.

Failure is funny stuff. If we're fixated with success we're usually allergic to failure, unless it's of the how-are-the-mighty-fallen-told-you-he-had-feet-of-clay variety.

Anthony McGowan is a writer (*memento mori*, Tony, *memento mori*). His first book, *Stag Hunt,* was published by Hodder and Stoughton in 2004. Yet his route to being an author was one of turbulent rejection. He wrote of this eloquently in *The Times* colour supplement of 20 March 2004:

> *'Failure comes in many forms: personal, professional, moral. Businesses fail, marriages fail, hopes fail. There are earnest strivers who can't quite just make it; there are public school masters who can't be bothered; there are mad jabberers who are at least denied the knowledge of their own failure. But however your failure is served up nothing adds quite so much to its sting as the proximity of dazzling success.'*

Boy, oh boy, does Anthony know about failure. He's got a PhD in it. How about this?

> *'I was pitied but also feared. Everyone knows that failure contaminates and I had the Ebola strain.'*

It's true. If you're a gambler you avoid unlucky people. You know the ones. They trip over things. They just miss trains. They lack what that advertising doyen of the 70s, Peter Marsh, described as 'restaurant presence', that ineffable ability to catch the maître d's eye at two dozen paces, to be served first, to be the restaurant focal point. Like Napoleon, who in response to being asked if he wanted successful generals replied, 'No, give me lucky ones.'

Failure is a disease. They say 'success breeds success', but while we're about clichés how about 'failure is a super-virus in any organization'?

It's not the 'didn't work out' thing about failure that matters, it's the threefold consequence:

(i)   the denial (this worst of all – no chance of doing any learning if this happens);

(ii) the fear of further failure (leading to hesitant demands to have more information than is necessary to make a decision or, worse still, a reckless 'let's just go for it with our eyes closed' attitude spawned from terror); or

(iii) finally, that worst of all state of mind – apathy, and an inability, disinclination or fatigue in determining what is good or bad, what is successful or a failure.

Failure when it's expected has a dreadfully contaminating impact on all those around the person emanating it.

The very worst of this contaminating failure phenomenon lies in older executives whose self-belief and optimism have evaporated. Not so much 'is the glass half full or half empty?' as 'who cares if there's a glass anyway?' Jill Garrett of the mentoring company Caret told me of an earlier experience in her life when she was a head teacher and she faced this kind of '*negative fatalism*':

> '*They were department heads. They were not incompetent so I couldn't fire them. They were not lazy. So ditto. But they'd given up the will to live as I know it. They had, as it were, gone out.*'

Negative fatalism is a common virus. Its symptoms are doing the least possible to get away with your job, a dismissive attitude towards your customers, an expectation that things will turn out badly and the preparation of plausible excuses to cover this outcome.

One other thing. It's highly contagious.

So what happened to Anthony McGowan? Did he just get lucky or did he apply himself? Did he, in short, fix the puncture and get on his bike?

It's not (as he says himself) quite as simple as that. As any writer knows, one day the muse is with you, the next you couldn't write yourself out of a paper bag. Inspiration is fickle – and success in a highly subjective area like novel-writing is quite a bit to do with luck.

But it's also to do with hope. And with striving. And with maintaining a cheerful disposition about life. The problem with failure isn't failure itself. It's the conspirators that make it happen who are so dreary and self-centred in their having failed to pull it off. There's a kind of 'I told you so' about a lot of failure.

Follow the advice of Reichheld. Analyze every failure to death, every little detail – remorselessly. You'll be surprised at what you come up with. As he observes, the average sports coach doesn't spend the Monday and Thursday after the big match gloating over the highlights. He's nitpicking over the failures, trying to work out how to eliminate the mistakes that spoilt the way the team performed. He'll be looking for examples of systemic weakness, for easily changed lapses, for patterns of error. Six Sigma is a management tool that is designed to help management to do just this. It is based on the premise that it is *inconsistency of delivery* that is the real killer, the real source of most failure.

Reichheld notes there is one service that consistently (thank God) beats the holy grail of Six Sigma. The airline industry. And when a crash does happen they have a black box that they rip open to discover exactly what happened, why it happened, when it happened, how it happened and, most importantly, how to ensure it doesn't happen again.

Hurray for black boxes. Time we installed metaphorical black boxes in every department of every business. Time we installed them in our own psyches too.

But I doubt if we'll eliminate the obsession with success. It's too primal and it's quite simply too much fun.

For me the big lessons here are:

1. Never be defensive about failure. Admit it and analyze it. Work out why what went wrong went wrong.

2. Avoid the word 'failure'. Actors when they fail to get a part say they are 'resting'. So when things don't work out for you quite as you'd hoped, go into *thinking mode.*

3. Avoid people who suck out your energy. Do not work with cynics or depressives if you can avoid it. Pick out optimists and life lovers and join their team.

4. Aim for consistency of performance and behaviour – the biggest failing in the current world is to be described as unreliable.

5. When looking at problems, do as Einstein urged and 'invert' – see things from opposite viewpoints.

6. Write this on your hand: '*I am here to learn*'.

11 Knowing When to Quit

Knowing when to say 'enough' is a liberating experience. Realizing that you, are on your own, only one component in achieving break-through is a big step towards success. So too is securing your exit and your successor.

'No man is an island, entire of itself; every man is a piece of the continent, a part of the main; if a clod be washed away by the sea, Europe is the less, as well if a promontory were, as well as if a manor of thy friends or of thine own were; any man's death diminishes me, because I'm involved in mankind; and therefore never send to know for whom the bell tolls; it tolls for thee.'

John Donne
Devotions upon Emergent Occasions, Meditation 17, 1624

'... you've got to know when to hold them, know when to fold them ...'

Kenny Rogers

MOVE IN. MOVE ON. MOVE OUT.

Getting out at the right time has never been easy. Nearly all executives leave it too late or fail to recognize the omens. Sir Philip Watts would have done better resigning from Shell two (months? years? decades?) before he was sacked. Luc van der Velde hung on too long at Marks & Spencer (history will judge how far too long). Even Jack Welch was too reluctant to go from GE.

So let's get this straight.

Just as one thing is certain, that if you are born you are also going to die, so you should be planning your departure the same day you join your company, the very second you begin a new job. Sounds drastic, maybe, but unless you set a plan in place things will drift and you and everyone will one day face a tricky and embarrassing situation.

Go back a decade or so and the following were all true.

People had jobs for life.

It was important to have a *proper* 9–5 job. Freelance or portfolio was not nice unless you were a journalist (which was not very nice either).

You got promoted *very slowly*. If you were doing well you'd be a senior manager by the time you were 30, on the board at 40, MD at 50, chairman at 60, retire at 65 or maybe even 70. All this – except in advertising, where the ages of promotion were 9, 14, 17, 20 and 25 (no, I'm joking, but they were always a lot younger. I was on the board of my agency well before I was 30, and that was a long time ago).

Everyone earned *about the same* – headmasters, permanent secretaries, directors of banks, finance directors of manufacturing companies. The perks in the City and media were good but the tax regime meant what you earned wasn't really that important.

Entrepreneurialism was for a dubious few. Being an entrepreneur was a bit spivvy. A bit 'retail' – like, say, being a Gerald Ronson or Phil Green.

A decent *education* ensured a decent career.

Where you came from determined where you went.

You only got fired for being dishonest or extraordinarily incompetent, seldom for being surplus to requirements, being past it or being lazy. (In Japan, when your usefulness to a company lessened they used to promote you to a 'seat by the window' where the light was better and you could read the small print of a newspaper more easily.)

You worked *abroad* only on a temporary basis and then with some reluctance. It was like being seconded to a far-flung part of the Empire.

This all discouraged mobility of labour. People didn't change jobs or move homes or their neighbourhood. I knew people who'd literally never left Northampton where they'd been born. Never even been to Towcester or Milton Keynes. Imprisoned in their own comfort zone. So there was no need to move on except when you died or retired, and even then you were likely to stay put. Now is very different. And it's disturbing a lot of people, not least the Archbishop of Canterbury, Rowan Williams, who calls this a *carpe diem* society in which we carelessly discard what we've experienced and move on. This includes partners and religion.

We shall have, we're told by futurologists, three relationships before we die, twenty jobs, ten homes, live on at least two continents. Promiscuity will be the norm. Like as not we'll go from being an investment banker to a teacher to a plumber to an entrepreneur to a charity worker. Neither good nor bad at anything, just a sampler of all. *We'll move on before we get found out.*

Well, that's a cynical view, and no doubt Rowan Williams has a point about the instability of modern relationships, personal and working. Yet to make a huge, committed contribution to something, only moving on to do more good work somewhere else when you realize your contribution has peaked, seems a pretty good way of behaving.

Serge Trigano, who used to run Club Med, reckoned in the 1980s that the optimum period a person could consistently contribute to a job was about ten years, with the real peak at around five or six years.

So how do you plan your exit? *Two ways.*

1. Make it totally transparent and embedded in the constitution of your business. We've done this recently at our charity, Shaftesbury Homes and Arethusa. Previously, trustees served in perpetuity. They now serve two five-year terms. One trustee remarked to me rather grimly as he acceded to the idea that it was, from his perspective, like 'turkeys voting for Christmas'. Yet the benefit is that we have to constantly seek new trustees who bring new skills to us. And those of us with relatively little time left to serve are impelled to ensure we maximize the difference we make to the organization before we go. Everyone knows where they are (or in the case of those who've served more than ten years, where they aren't).

2. Write a personal business plan, which probably comprises two five-year periods with a personal review every six months. You create your own milestones and objectives. You modify these as events conspire to change how you're doing. The difference between this and scenario 1 is that this one is *very, very private*. Private it may be, but it represents the most vigorous renunciation of 'Que sera, sera' imaginable. And about time. The biggest misery in life is usually caused by timidity in grasping the nettle.

Decide that it's time to go. Leave all your affairs in good order, sort out the handover. Be unemotional and responsible, like David Abbott was when he retired from AMV BBDO. This will leave you feeling great, grown up and fine.

By the way, do try to avoid this word 'fine' – it doesn't mean what you think. When people say between clenched teeth in response to the question 'How are you?', ' I'm fine, thanks,' they usually mean the reverse. As Dr Bartholomew Sayle tells us, 'fine' equals

F – f***ed up

I – insecure

N – neurotic

E – emotional.

So anyway, after that digression, you leave your business feeling *fine* and it may be *fine* for you, but how about the organization you are leaving?

Are you leaving it in good or abandoned shape?

Who is your successor? If you've been as good at your job as you'd hoped you'd been, you'll have sorted out a smooth handover (whether you are CEO or brand manager) to someone *you expect will be better than you.*

(That thought hurts most people. Well, we are human aren't we?)

Define 'smooth'.

It means:

1. *Comprehensive briefing notes.*

2. Summary of all the *current issues.*

3. Summary of all the *strategic issues.*

4. Write-up on all the *stakeholders* – their agenda, the quality of the relationship with the company and specifically with you, what they have to offer, where they are going.

5. *A filing system* that works – less important the more senior you are; someone else will be in charge of this usually, but if it's been your brainchild then make sure it works for your successor.

6. Two intensive *Q & A sessions* so your successor can really quiz you.

What else?

It means QUICK.

When you are going to go, go. Don't hang about. Don't be like Clive Thompson of Rentokil, of whom it was said by his fellow director and successor as chairman, Brian McGowan,

> *'Sir Clive's presence was so all-pervading that to change the culture of the business was impossible. We decided to liberate the company from its past.'*

We shall see what happens, but that is not the epitaph most of us would wish for ourselves. Far better to be the one in charge, such as Martin Johnston, Nasser Hussain or even Alistair Campbell, and leave elegantly (or at any rate independently) under your own steam with your organization left in responsible and fine working order. Most people, such as Jimmy Young, Michael Parkinson, Margaret Thatcher, Peter Bonfield, tend to be led extremely reluctantly from the battlefield.

The true meaning of a successful person is not in their longevity of tenure but in the effectiveness of what they did and their ability to read correctly the moment to depart.

Financiers are keen on talking about 'exit strategies'. Careerists should be just as keen, as it's just as important.

Remember Malcolm's words in Macbeth:

Nothing in his life
Became him like the leaving it; he died
As one that had been studied in his death
To throw away the dearest thing he owed
As 'twere a careless trifle.

Liberate yourself. Throw it away. Be a change artist, not a hanger-on.

Four final words of advice.

1. Don't go earlier than is necessary to achieve what is needed. Never leave your colleagues in the lurch.

2. Encourage everyone in your business to be skilled succession planners. Who will take over from them? When they get to see this is a good thing to do, you and they are on the way to designing a really brilliant and robust company.

3. If you are encouraging a 'do the job brilliantly and then move on' culture, you need to work with an executive search business so they can bring you and your colleagues new opportunities in due course. It's an interesting brief.

4. Do not allow the concept of there being a time limit on employment to do anything other than put urgency into the doing of it. A job is not a place to go. It's a thing to get done.

12 You Don't Have to be Original to Succeed

It's all about being better, about not being hard to pigeonhole or being different just for different's sake.

'Amateurs borrow. Professionals steal.'

Pablo Picasso

'Anyone who claims to be truly original has no memory.'

Coco Chanel

BETTER BEATS UNIQUE

It must seem strange for someone who spent a good part of his life in advertising to be so dismissive of originality. Damon Collins, the creative director of Lowe, said,

> *'you are not as good as the last ad you did but as good as the next ad you are going to do ... and just how scary is that?'*

Well, Damon, I can think of scarier. There was much scarier stuff in *I'm a Celebrity, Get Me Out of Here*. Doing anything creative has a certain frisson to it that that blank sheet of paper creates in the 'ideas blocked' mind, but *scary*? No, I don't think so.

In the world of business we tend to overestimate the role of originality in achieving success. Very often 'original' is too extreme and beyond the current appetite of the market. I am reminded of the horror with which Jim Hacker in *Yes, Minister* greets the remark 'Well, Minister, if I may say so, that's a very courageous step to take.'

Courageous is not smart in politics, just as *original* is not always smart in business. To be described as 'original' is, after all, to be defined as 'eccentric'.

Better by far to follow Picasso and do what most really successful new businesses do: 'adapt and improve'. Is Starbuck's original? Is Pret A Manger original? Is Gap or Top Shop original? All of them are an idea that is needed, done better. Alexander Pope got it right:

What oft was thought but ne'er so well expressed.

In that lies the true, solid centre ground of success for most commercial organizations. All too often we see someone with an idea that is probably quite smart but is unfortunately inexplicable. *No, that's not fair.* It's explicable to the explainer but incomprehensible to the listener.

'Hmm. What would you say this product idea of yours is like? Who is your nearest competitor?'

'There is no real competitor. The idea is unique.'

Oh, dear. So is a three-headed frog. Not much demand for those either (unless you are a biologist or editor of the *Sun*, I suppose ... actually, three-headed frogs sound a whole lot more popular than the average 'unique' business idea).

Success lies more often in being in a clear, understandable pigeonhole – banking, marketing, consultancy, whatever – and being very clear what you can and can't do and being passionately committed to and successful in being outstanding in that slot.

Don't believe Homer Simpson, who said,

'If you think you're good at something there are a million people out there better at it than you.'

It's just not true.

It really isn't.

In a given slot (and it may be a small one defined by geography, price, specialism) you, yes, you, have the potential gift of superiority. What you are less likely to have is the gift of originality. (And be praised for that.)

The disadvantages of originality appear below. They should deter you from this dangerous world even if this aphorism doesn't:

'Pioneers tend to get scalped – better travel in convoy.'

Original	Tried/Tested
Unfamiliar	Understood
Uncomfortable	Safe
Unproven	Proved
Expensive	Value for money
May not be needed	Constantly in use
No benchmark	Capable of being improved

No discussion of originality would seem complete without considering that major contribution to road safety, the C5.

No, not the most recent car from Citroën, who rather abjectly nicked the name of the notorious Sinclairmobile.

Sir Clive Sinclair and the C5

What an extraordinary man ... never seen someone almost bald but with red hair, a kind of mature Chris Evans, the manic eyes of a Mensa genius, the sexual reputation of a biblical hero (well, he always had a gorgeous girl draped on his arm – not original but very creative) ... never met someone who fell quite so squarely in the phrase 'nice idea, shame about the execution'. Here was 'good in theory, didn't work in practice' incarnate.

The C5 was an electric car. It was like the cockpit of a Spitfire on three half-concealed wheels. You had automotive controls apart from the steering, which you did by adjusting a bar under your legs (yes, actually under your thighs).

I got one of these death traps in the late 1980s on thirty days' approval. I actually drove it down Baker Street in the rush hour. Nearly came to grief in a pothole (the sort you don't notice in a car but in the C5 was like descending into a quarry and nearly capsizing). It was certainly the most frightening experience of my life – Dracula at nightfall in a Transylvanian forest is a pussy cat by comparison. Give me cyanide but don't ask me to commit C5 suicide again. Mind you, I did get a lot of laughs – mainly from bus drivers trying to knock me off the road as they whistled 'Pinball Wizard'.

The C5 was not an idea ahead of its time. It was an idea ahead of sanity, ahead of any human need. But it was *original*. Most mystifying about it was the sheer amateurism of its manufacturer. It screamed prototype at you (they say another ghastly failure – the De Lorean – did the same thing. You couldn't even touch the De Lorean. Brushed steel attracts smudgy fingerprints, you see).

Sir Clive was evidently not stupid. But he was surrounded by terrible engineers or executioners of his vision. If this derided idea had been developed and produced by the Japanese it might even have been a success. At least it might have felt safe.

Back for a moment to the world of advertising that I rebuked at the beginning of this chapter. To the real craftsmen of the business – the Abbotts, Hegartys and Brignulls – the question was seldom 'is it original?' so much as 'does it work in a new and fresh way?'

The need for 'new' and 'fresh' was quite simply the perceived need not to be the same-old telling a heard-before story. Smart thinking that, if you wanted to cut through the white noise that started filling our heads in the later years of the twentieth century.

Before my time at FCO Richard French and Ian Potter created the Araldite campaign – the famous car stuck to a poster with the line 'It also sticks handles to teapots'. It won loads of awards. It cheered up lots of people. It was brilliant. As near to original as you get, but most of all it was a particularly wonderful way of selling strong glue. The campaign generated much more PR and noise than it cost in media; it even featured in the Russian newspaper *Isvestia*, which commented,

> *'The lengths to which capitalists go to sell cars.'*

Interesting, isn't it, how ideologues often miss the point?

So how would we really judge this advertising now in the cold light of the twenty-first century?

Original	– *yes*
Creative	– *certainly*
Newsworthy	– *absolutely*
Successful	– *Hmm!*

Depends on how you define that last word. Won awards, got lots of envious glances from our peers, maybe even sold quite of lot of tubes of the stuff.

As the client fired us right at the height of the advertising's success (I'd arrived by then), he said they felt the advertising was 'rather arrogant'. I remember trying to reason with him when in fact the only sensible course of action was to punch him – very hard.

I'm not sure if Araldite exists nowadays and if it does I obviously wouldn't buy it, but what in retrospect was so delicious about this experience was the sheer ineptitude of trying to fit this unambitious client with a splendid cashmere suit when all he came in for was a pair of dungarees. As the creative gurus of the world poured praise upon his unwilling, hunched shoulders you could almost hear him in mock Graham Norton tones protesting, 'All I asked was to increase our distribution.'

And that's what creativity is like in the world of commerce. It's hard to quantify the real effect of most advertising whatever they tell you, and sadly the most reliable data is based on how much people spend, not how well they tell their sales story.

If the real barometer of success is sales then come on down the following stars of advertising:

Shake 'n' Vac

esure

Ferrero Rocher

Success comes from drilling a name into as many people's brains as possible.

We also live in a world (but don't tell *Campaign*, the advertising magazine) where the old-fashioned communications model has been broken and is irreparable. Because there's

too much media.

too many ads.

too many different consumers.

too many products.

consumers too smart for the advertiser's good ('don't worry, dear, it's only a commercial').

And Michael Winner is right. It *is* only a commercial, and the way to be heard in a cavernous nightclub isn't with the kind of polite coughs that interrupted our middle-class lives in the 1970s (Heineken, Hamlet, Guinness and so on).

We have, in short, stopped being so polite.

In the hustle and bustle of the twenty-first century 'polite' is a luxury. One of the most imposing and successful folk heroes of the current world is Gordon Ramsay (pause to swear, shout and scratch your arse) who f***ing tells these w*****s who can't cook where the f***ers f***ing get off. Got it?)

In a world where Ramsay is in, polite is definitely out.

No, what's actually in isn't Gordon Ramsay. It's what was always in. Different is in. Different is what I learned in advertising. Or, as that urbane practitioner Robin Wight rather laconically suggested, 'When the others zig you zag.'

To succeed you have to stand out – just enough, not too much. To be exceptional or be seen as such, you have to be comparable. 'What's black and white and eats like a horse?' Yes, it's a zebra. But you don't have to be a zebra to stand out. Zebras, you see, are herd animals that hate being separated from their mates. They are also very bad-tempered, with a very short attention span. Yet one of the Rothschilds managed to harness two to a carriage and drive through the New Forest. Much better to have a very fast horse. At least you know where you are.

Don't try to be too original. Do, however, be different.

13 Why Women can be so Successful

Success shouldn't be a lottery if you are a woman (and you'll regret it if you don't make the most of what life has to offer ...)

Dianne Thompson – some lessons from a success.

'the good not done, the love not given, time torn off unused'

Philip Larkin

IN PRAISE OF WOMEN

Dianne Thompson's dad was a butcher. Incredibly hard-working, focused and fun. He sounds terrific. He is her role model and friend – she adores taking him away on trips – lucky both of them. She puts her work ethic and determination down to his inspiration. But when I ask her for her definition of success it isn't so much a British as an American-sounding one I get: 'To exceed the expectations of my stakeholders.'

I've always thought in Britain, where we suffer from such low standards in the service sector, that any marketer talking about 'exceeding consumer expectation and delighting them' was in fact talking apirational guff. *In the end, just meeting expectations would be pretty impressive.* Yet Dianne's point is deeply personal and valid:

> *'To stand up there and say, for instance, "We are back in growth at Camelot a year ahead of forecast ..." fills one with satisfaction. Inside, there's a little smirk and a real wish to shout "Yes".'*

The ultimate competitor in me warms to this, to define success as a display of 'I showed them: they didn't think I could but I did; I *won*'. King, or in this case, queen of the castle stuff.

I described this as an American-sounding definition, by which I meant it had the hard edge of 'superachiever' to it. A clarity of focus we supposedly less ambitious and more laid-back Brits so often seem to lack.

Success is something Dianne has tasted at Camelot, most vividly in retaining the Lottery franchise when the ubiquitous and bearded Sir Richard Branson nearly scooped it away, until an ex-Permanent Secretary of the Treasury, Sir Terry Burns, was brought in to replace the chair of the board arbitrating over the tender process. He judged the merits of the bids and sent Sir Richard packing. More importantly, he gave a massive vote of confidence to Dianne.

Success is something she regards not as hers of right but something to be worked for, something earned. She speaks only fleetingly of luck (which is strange, given the sector she works in), wonders if there are lucky people, suspects that merely thinking you are lucky and continuing to do so will itself bring good fortune, says how well things are going for her and then touches wood for luck. *She believes in luck.*

Successful formulae? She has strategic insights into any number of companies that she rattles off convincingly but says with gravity that execution really is king, that of all her regrets it's been that sometimes she hasn't done things better. She puts down the Camelot recovery story to 'A hundred or so things all being done 10 per cent better.'

Ten per cent? I think she is being modest, but she is adamantly opposed to the grand 'in-one-jump-Jack-was-free strategy'. She is a living advertisement for careful crafting and old-fashioned engineering values. It's interesting that Jack Welch was an engineer, and so were a lot of the great American industrialists. Odd that so few people are nowadays. Engineer craftsman rather than MBA whizzkid feels a lot more convincing.

Tom Peters talks about the 'feminine advantage'. Dianne has it. She's smart. She's focused. She's determined. But she's also very sensitive in a way her male peers seldom are. She'd be a compassionate executioner.

Why should women have this advantage? Is it genetic? They are blessed with a series of advantages:

1. They are great *jugglers* – it goes with the genes. They are designed to cope in a 'do this, do that' world where crisis is the norm.

2. They are by definition *team builders*, creators of families rather than lone hunters. In the current world the lone hunter is an outdated species.

3. They are incredibly *protective* of their own.

4. They have a *determination* the more flexible male often lacks. Would the charming Ian Gilmour have stood up to the unions like Margaret Thatcher did? Chirac shows by his vapid inactivity how lacking in balls most male leaders are, despite their posturing as being testicular and strong.

5. *They listen.*

6. They have better *risk/reward* antennae. Margaret Thatcher again … reputation: decisive, even impulsive. In reality, she was very prudent and perhaps overly cautious.

7. They tend to be more *philosophical* about things going wrong and focus on solving the problem rather than blaming anyone.

8. They tend to be more *patient* than men.

9. *They respect professionalism.*

10. *They know when they're licked* and when they're not. (Example of licked: Barbara Cassani and the Olympic bid. Example of not yet licked: Dianne Thompson and the Lottery bid when she knew she *wasn't* … although everyone else thought she was.)

Patience seems an odd strength, but it lies in the fact that women often tend to be phlegmatic about how long things take to happen. They are good at detail (usually) and they sense the fact that you can't rush things like cooking. They tend not to go for 'microwave management', unlike their male counterparts. Nor do they go for that other great flaw of today's executive, which is to stay remote from people and indulge in 'air-conditioned thinking'. These are nappy-changers, for heaven's sake.

Dianne Thompson is realistic about how long things take, but she's uncharacteristically tetchy about things taking an unnecessarily long time to do or being overly complex.

And there's a lot more to do.

She rattles off a series of 'could have done better at' relating to previous jobs. But at Camelot she feels comfortable; she's built a great team that is well aligned, motivated and hungry.

Success, she says, is also about building and leading a team. Not just leading them but providing them with the urge to do better. *Accept that there is no perfect solution, that you can always improve, and you may be on the verge of understanding what success really might be.*

So that triumphant inner 'yes!' I talked about earlier is followed by a 'yes, but …', because the urge to do better and better and better has to burn in you if you are to be truly a sustained success.

Sir Clive Woodward, unremarkably, has pretty strong views on this. He's spoken inspiringly to Dianne's management group about the steps to success. One of these steps is what is called 'teamship'.

Remember that the England team, apart from being talented at rugby, are also young and inexperienced in the ways of life. Curiously small issues of protocol, small to you and me, cause them anxiety (think of young people you know. To them little things mean a lot). We're talking protocol, clothes rules, all sorts of stuff. Apparently the squad produced a comprehensive and detailed 'teamship' manual to which every member had to sign up honouring the pledge to conform to these agreed 'teamship' rules. Anyone can raise an issue and say, 'I think we can improve this one,' and provided he sells this to the rest of the squad it will be adopted, subject to the OK of Sir Clive who retains the power of ultimate veto.

It's the concept of meticulous and assiduously detailed planning that appeals so much. No empty rhetoric here. No high-sounding but empty bombast. Sport really has moved to a new level.

The other thing Sir Clive has changed is the celebration of success. Which is not really needed because you *expect* to win. So no longer is there the 'did we really pull that off?' beer-soaked macho victory party. But if they lose there is a huge bonding – *how* do we change, what *really* went wrong, *where* and *what* were the failure issues? This is a time to recollect and reflect and emerge better informed and stronger. Since the World Cup success there's lots of beer-drinking then. Only goes to show, as John Hegarty, the advertising genius, said to me, 'you can't let your eye wander for a minute … you have to keep on top of it'.

So in this fast-moving, better-informed world things must be getting better.

'No, I'm afraid they aren't ...'

Dianne looks and sounds rueful about this. To be sure, she concedes a few people may be getting better, but overall the same malaise of inadequate capital investment, poor understanding of the need to invest and a worse recognition of how to coach and develop people still exists. There are exceptions, such as Walmart. They stand out through their great systems and investment in technology. The good aren't good just because they are talented (an old British misconception), they are good because they know where to invest their cash in the effort to stay ahead.

Consistency is more important than erratic brilliance.

Is that really true? *One hundred per cent, totally, incontrovertibly*. It may well be that consistency of performance will be the one thing we hold up as the key to sustained success in the twenty-first century.

Or in Dianne Thompson's case a consistency of performance that exceeds the stakeholder expectation day in and day out.

Success doesn't come in spurts, it's a long, long growth curve. It does need patience and it does need constant vigilance and hands-on management. It's a 24/7 business, being a leader: 'you get married to the job, I suppose'.

It seems a pretty happy marriage and a very interesting one, without anyone taking anything for granted.

Success is not a lottery if you plan and work at it hard enough. Most of it revolves around being two things.

A realist and a pragmatist.

This doesn't mean the visionary stuff is irrelevant, just that it is the last thing that matters. But typically Dianne, Veuve Cliquot Businesswoman of the Year a couple of years back, has a flaw. Too modest. The success gene her parents gave her plus the bit of magic she added – fierce, almost frightening, determination – have made the difference.

Dianne is really good. Talk to the people who work for her to find out. Talk to virtually anyone (should anyone be this popular?). But she's also quite tough.

Successes usually are quite tough.

14 Success is Wonderful

Personal success. Public pressure. The story of a triple achiever who's kept true to himself despite his recent downfall.

Sir Peter Davis

'Be what you is not what you ain't 'cos

if you ain't what you is you is what you ain't.'

Luther D. Price

Sir Peter Davis is a large, imposing, impressive, cuddly bear of a man. He listens to you – really listens – and is beautifully mannered. He replies promptly to your letters. He shows you to the lift when you leave his office, says goodbye properly. He is a gentleman, in the best sense of that word.

He is charming but has been badly hurt by the Sainsbury experience. When talking about his time there he lists Sainsbury's socially responsible achievements (fortieth company in the FTSE index in terms of market capitalization but fourth in terms of giving to charity. For four years running judged the best retailer in the environmental index). But he adds, 'that's not me ... that's really all part of the family tradition'.

It's impossible not to like him and warm to his, at times, boyish enthusiasm for the company he clearly adored and for his grasp of detail. He knows the layout, location, problems and issues of all Sainsbury stores much as a cricket-mad 11-year-old knows *Wisden* by heart.

Sir Peter is a success.

Exceedingly well off, titled, with a family of which he is clearly proud and whose own success he regards with affection. A man liked, rated and enjoyed by all those around him. You can hear it coming, can't you, like the roar of flood water coming down an alleyway ... *but* ... *BUT* ... *BUT*.

What has gone wrong?

Here's one for the record books. It's mighty impressive. Sir Peter is the *only guy ever* to have been CEO of three FTSE 50 companies all in different sectors (Reed Elsevier, the Prudential, Sainsbury's). He's been a CEO, with a brief gap after Reed, for eighteen years and an FTSE board member for twenty-seven years.

A success. A huge success.

But ... Sainsbury's has been a major disappointment to his shareholders, to the media, to the staff and most poignantly to him. This glittering career has culminated in public failure. Fair?

As John Neill said, it's all about context. The good news for the group is it's outperformed the FTSE by 52 per cent under his stewardship (no, please don't ask about Tesco and Morrison). It's clawed back lost customers. Customers' views of Sainsbury's have improved significantly on all fronts except price. There's been a massive investment programme. All just in time for his successor as CEO to reap the benefits. Yet the numbers are dwarfed by the juggernaut Tesco and the Yorkshire sledgehammer Morrison. Like M&S, for which Peter was also headhunted post-Greenbury, Sainsbury's has been under a censorious investor limelight.

In his presence you are impressed by his ability to combine focus, energy and calm – that's one hell of a cool juggling act – and almost conceal his anguish that this swansong has turned into a dismissal for a duck and certainly not the valedictory paean he'd hoped for and deserved.

Was it his fault? He possesses a magic touch. This was the man who turned the shambling mess of Reed into a pure play media business, who put integrity and order back into the Prudential after their mis-selling crisis, and who immediately on his return to Sainsbury's put a smile back on to the collective face of his staff and shareholders. Here was a man who knew the company, knew his stuff and clearly enjoyed life. A two-trolley shopper. *He really was the sort of person who could taste the difference.*

The legacy was hard to deal with. Massive underinvestment in systems. A management looking backwards and not forwards. Paranoia about the advance of Tesco. Sir Peter is generous about his predecessors, and takes what's happened and not happened on the chin:

> '*I underestimated the task. I was flattered to be asked, as it were, to come home. I had been told I'd never get this job. Maybe I took it for the wrong reasons. But I certainly underestimated it.*'

Ironically, he thought he was *coming back into his comfort zone*. In fact, he was comfortable and in familiar territory, and took too long, far longer than he as a stranger would have done, to spot and deal with all the symptoms of decay.

Lesson: Don't be too nice.

Lesson: Do stuff with ruthless energy. A few symbolic hangings always help. To be fair, he did those.

Lesson: Don't make emotional decisions about jobs (yes, I know, nearly everyone we know has done this). It's business, not personal.

Sir Peter says ruefully – just a week before he left Sainsbury's – as he looked over Holborn from his small office in what was once Robert Maxwell's HQ (the monster Maxwell would not have tolerated such moderation in office status, although he could have said this with far greater reason than Sir Peter): 'I think I've taken and been too prepared to take risks with my own career.'

Prescient words. A week later he was proved right. Was anything worth the opprobrium heaped on him ahead of the Sainsbury AGM?

I glanced at a picture of his yacht on the wall, mentally totting up his income (in common, as it turned out, with most of Fleet Street) and think, 'some risk, some reward'.

But, of course, he's right. That's only money. Money can't buy you love.

And this lovable man wanted more than anything else to have won the battle of the supermarkets for his shareholders. Sure – he's not stupid, that's his remit to his shareholders as CEO or Chairman – but perhaps more especially he wanted to do it for his staff because there's nothing better than to manage a winning team (ask Sir Clive Woodward). It was also because it was his dream from first time round, when he was Assistant MD in the late 1970s.

Unfulfilled dreams are tough to take. As taking unfulfilment goes, he's doing wonderfully well. He is gracious about his competitors and his critics. And totally realistic.

What would he change?

No regrets?

There's a slightly weary sense he exudes momentarily of having been on a highly exposed treadmill for a very long time. He talks about his three children, his sons – one a corporate, one an entrepreneur – and his daughter, who studied event management. They perfectly reflect Peter himself. Tripartite. Corporate politician. Risk-taker. Showman. He winces. Too glib, perhaps, and he doesn't much like glib. Urbane, yes. Glib, no.

He regrets some of the trends that make being a CEO in the UK more taxing than perhaps it should be:

☆ Putting things back into society is spoken of warmly, but he regrets that in truth few really successful companies do it.

☆ Hedge funds and derivatives account for a huge amount of stock market activity. Well, do you understand them? And should this influence how companies are run?

☆ Small investors make a huge amount of noise and cause great trouble. (I remember one such oxymoron of a man – he was called Hero – in the Saatchi fiasco.)

But, he confesses finally, this has all been fun. Success has been hard work. Success has been a trap – how do you get off the treadmill? His plans to get off and run his own business were interrupted by calls of duty, security and wealth. But perhaps he missed out … he's too good to waste his time on politics (he reflects ruefully on the latter days at Reed Elsevier: 'That was horrible.' On reflection, he may decide this is worse) and still too energetic to be in the back seat. He says at his age the energy wears thin. But he is trying it on. He's got plenty of fuel in the tank.

He's such a nice guy I really wish it hadn't ended like this. And do you know, having myself known him for nearly thirty-five years he really hasn't changed. In fact, his success suited him a lot.

I really hope we haven't seen the last of him. He will emerge in a senior role in charity, government advisory work or something he really enjoys, such as chairman of a great boatbuilding company or a restaurant chain – sad for his previous employer that his love of food and improving standards didn't translate into the numbers.

Interesting for all of us aspiring to success that this great example of success was ultimately tumbled.

Memento mori, Peter, *memento mori*.

15 Bloody-minded Determination

There is no way of insuring success other than Bloody-minded Determination and a bit of luck. A conversation with a bright, young success for whom this is just the beginning of the journey.

Mike Kirsch

'Now is the winter of our discontent made glorious summer by this son of York'

Richard III, *Shakespeare*

IN PRAISE OF AMBITION

York is old, very British and quaint. A cross between Oxford and Canterbury. The Minster is a staggering piece of architecture just about held together by inventive excavation and support systems.

It reminds me of many corporations.

The astonishing stained glass was delivered in the thirteenth century against a series of agreed KPIs (Key Performance Indicators) and the designer, Ivo de Raghton, earned in modern-day terms around £750,000 for just less than two years' excellent work, most of it on bonus.

York feels rich. York is about profit. Not least when you visit Norwich Union. It feels rich, profitable and, most of all, successful.

And success, as Mike Kirsch's bright son Richard observed, follows money:

'Don't expect anyone to do a huge amount if there isn't a profit in it.'

He says this late at night, heavy with a cold, having come down for a glass of water as we debate the potential fuel crisis in Saudi Arabia and the alternatives to oil. He thinks any fuels bar nuclear are goers provided enough government cash goes into them.

Out of the mouths of ... Richard is fifteen. He's clever. He's self-assured. He's nice. He's impressive. He is a great advertisement for youth. I suggest to Judith and Mike that Mike retires. That he and Judith give *all* their money to Richard with the brief to multiply it tenfold. They demur. Love that word – demur. No, they actually say, 'Piss off. He has to do his GCSEs.'

Mike Kirsch used to be a client when I ran FCO. He was a brand manager at Booker and was responsible for Brewhurst, the healthfood wholesaling business. He was, I recall, an assertive and very energetic young man. Now, eighteen years later, he's travelled through Bryant & May, Amex, Lloyds TSB, Britannia Building Society, NatWest and now Norwich Union.

Aged forty-two, he's on the board of Britain's biggest life business. He's come a long way since peddling Allinson's wholemeal bread. He's an authority, a leading figure, an expert in a difficult area. Mike is, whichever way you look at it, a 'success'. And this is where the problem kicks in. He's in the premier league. As such, he's exposed to levels of criticism and expectation that are at best character-defining but at worst exhausting.

Quite simply, Mike is trapped (hard word, but it's one I got out of him and, even more reluctantly, out of Sir Peter Davis – that's how they both feel some of the time).

Trapped by the needs of his company: they obviously rate him – they should do.

Trapped by his own perceptions of what his family require of him.

Trapped by his own expectations: 'Well, you don't just stop do you? .... You carry on building a career ... doing things you never imagined you'd be asked to do.'

I'm fascinated by this. Mike's family background didn't confer a certainty of corporate success upon him. His father was a docker. Judith's, his wife, was a miner. Clear to me from what they say that both, in their own way and in their own terms, were successes – as I keep on saying, 'success is about being good and happy at what you do' – but neither would necessarily have expected to have bred these disciples of Mammon. Mike is a success but the urge, the need, the urgent itch to *exceed* not just *succeed* is enormous.

Why?

Maybe in Mike Kirsch we'll get nearer to understanding the 'need to succeed' than we have elsewhere.

I take assiduous notes as he talks, but find my mind wandering. I doubt if the story he's telling me is true. No. He's not lying. He just hasn't quite worked it out himself:

> *'An inner urge to succeed … a need to improve … busy is the only thing that matters … I can't bear lying in at the weekend.'*

The truth of the matter is that Mike is constantly pinching himself to keep himself awake in this nirvana of success. He's achieving stuff he never imagined he would or could. So when he says his role models are Margaret Thatcher and Gorbachev I obviously look askance enough for him to notice and say, 'Why not?' I'm surprised it isn't a Jack Welch or Chris Gent or Phil Green he's mentioned, but to Mike the scale of success has simply been more significant than an itsy-bitsy corporate turnaround or business success.

I ask him why he hasn't broken free from the corporate treadmill, as he's been so successful – why he hasn't done it all for himself. Hateful question. Not what any corporate success wants to be asked. But he shows his mettle:

> *'It's simple enough. If this is a treadmill I'm really good at treading it. Not by being a do-what-he's-told clone but by being myself. Why risk treading in space?'*

Mike has a clear and refreshing view about the need to be different. About the need to be able to say 'bollocks' (I have to confess this is a favourite word of mine – it has a certain crackle to it. Mike probably used it in an off-guard moment … so blame me if it's over the top). He wants to be himself, his own person, and put his head above the parapet. No business can flourish, we conclude, unless you hurl a variety of ingredients into the recipe.

So what is Mike? Worcester Sauce? Pepper? Garlic? Sure enough he isn't cream or yoghurt. He's smart enough to recognize that being cussed and different may one day spell disaster, but he passionately believes success has to come on his and Judith's terms, not *any* terms.

So long as he retains his self-confidence, that's fine. He describes how one former and bygone boss once managed to make Mike question his self-confidence. Hard to imagine that could ever happen, but bad leaders can do untold damage.

Big lesson: Your self-confidence is your biggest tool. Way ahead of brains. No wonder Jack Welch was such a fan of it. *If you don't feel good you almost certainly aren't going to be as good as you should be.*

Next big lesson: You may think you're doing fine, but if your boss doesn't think it too then you're not going to get very far. What Mike has learned to do is ask his boss regularly how things are going and to change his behaviour as required.

Success is a drug. Like nicotine – if you happen to be a smoker, you'll know what this means.

Success gets you. Just as you've made it – you're Phil Green – you've got BHS, Arcadia or whatever – when along comes the next lure: M&S. It's like fishing. There's always a bigger fish.

Because you never really make it – *however successful you are*. It's that old line about 'just one dollar more'. There are never enough dollars.

You never really become a 'master of the universe', just a more advanced apprentice.

The desire to move up the ladder becomes ever more acute. Retiring to the south of France is your brain's way of saying, 'enough is enough – this bar's gone high enough'. Mike is trapped on the ladder. The only way is up (the only safe way – you don't trust the rungs enough to go back down). The only appetite-quencher is more. And Mike, I suspect, has loads more to offer and is only just coming into his prime.

He talks about the need, the desire, the imperative for the *leadership* role. I tease him. I tell him this is his way of rationalizing the need for a one-more-success-cigarette, one more drag on the drug of 'you're doing really well, aren't you?'

'Leadership' is the big word – the one that all CEOs or CEOs-in-waiting use. Management is prosaic, watercolour stuff. Leadership is the real McCoy – oil painting. Leadership is in the world of Thatcher, Churchill, Elizabeth I, Jack Welch or – if you think about it – Attila the Hun and Hitler.

We talk about the success cocktail. Just six ingredients heartily shaken together:

market circumstance

competence

personality

hard work

timing

luck.

And I'd add just one other. Reading a book like this. More seriously ... *learning* from others.

No successful leader did it all by themselves.

Mike puts part of his own success down to the Norwich Union merger with Commercial Union which, as he describes it, 'completely reshuffled the deck'.

Like all effective operators, such reshuffling is something he welcomes.

So is success good?

You bet. 'Make the most of it ... enjoy it ... buy nice things ... take great holidays ... be successful in the way you live, enjoy the buzz.'

And just to pin this down ... is there more to it than those ingredients? Mike pauses and ponders and then says what he really thinks. Less glib and actually quite angry – no, not so much angry as assertive.

He *hates* other people's negativity. He *hates* the tendency to take it easy. He *hates* the propensity to take what turns up. Not to have goals. He *hates* the idea of ignoring the 'inner voice'. Most of all, he *hates* people who are not themselves.

Lesson: Fundamental to what he believes right, at his core is the vital need to be different, which is being yourself and being true to yourself. Be prepared to disagree (even to be disagreeable). Be happy to say 'bollocks'. Never, ever, just be a corporate clone.

So what is failure?

> MIKE: 'Losing self-respect, losing the respect of others, being weak, not addressing issues.'

> JUDITH: 'You haven't mentioned being right or wrong, Mike.'

They used to say that behind every successful man lay a successful woman. No, Judith, he didn't mention that, which is why he needs you.

It's a great question but a hard one. What's right on day one could be disastrous five years later (look at Marconi). It's a grey area and not one in which men are at their best. It's all to do with context.

Judith, however, played the 'feminine advantage' card. In ten years' time it'll be the Judiths of this world in the hot seat. No more glass ceilings.

'And no more wars.'

Why's that, Judith?

'Women hate war.'

Boudicca, Thatcher, Catherine the Great … ah, well.

And what if it's a just war? Or a war that benefits our babies? And gives us more oil? And … you see, it isn't that easy.

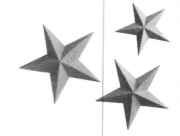

16 Being One Step Ahead

'I'm a success – get me out of here.' The most important thing in being a success in business is to be one step ahead and never work in a second rate place with second rate people – it'll rub off on you.

Peter Lederer OBE

'I think that success in business is about spotting talent, building people and helping them grow.'

Mervyn Davis, CEO of Standard Chartered Bank

IN PRAISE OF THE FUTURE

There's a verdant oasis in the middle of a well-watered paradise where the weather flexes its muscles, where the air is ripe with freshness, where the wealthy discard stress and play like children instead, where the list of things to do is endless and where time stops mattering, where infectious laughter is the norm, where real success is judged by the number of people smiling.

Gleneagles.

As you can see, I'm quite fond of the place. More than that ... I seriously believe it is the best-natured, best-run luxury leisure resort and hotel in the world. An outstanding, constantly awarded place owned by Diageo. It helps define world class in service and, like the Royal Bank of Scotland, Scottish excellence. It is consistently well managed with invention, spirit and aspiration.

Yet its harshest critic works there.

Peter Lederer OBE, who's been CEO for twenty years, says he doubts if Gleneagles is higher than twentieth in the world league of hotels, and says that twentieth would actually be a pretty good achievement.

Lesson: Be your own harshest critic. Never, ever, be complacent.

Success … what is it in a place like this?

I know how successful it is, and to have sustained such success in a difficult market largely empty of nervous post-9/11 American tourists is remarkable. Peter defines success in consumer terms:

> *'I would like every single guest to leave saying, "I spent more than I expected but it was worth every penny. Now I can't wait to go back. And I want to tell my friends about it."'*

Lesson: Be popular with people who give you their money and get them to recommend you.

And that's what a majority of guests do say and do feel. Not all of them, however. It's not so much Murphy's as McTaggart's law that says if you screw up with someone it's *always* the same guest. A bit like always hitting the same damaged finger with a hammer. Peter winces as he recalls getting it wrong and how no process can quite obviate that disaster waiting to happen. Orvis, of fishing rod fame, said to his staff,

> *'The customer's right even when he's goddammed wrong.'*

Of course. Always. For pragmatic reasons. Anyone in service must, as a matter of course, believe this. But, even so, imagine trying to keep one of the Gleneagles staff from attacking a guest (they do actually refrain from doing so, but envisage the inner turmoil) when they feel some upstart of a guest is totally unjustly impugning the integrity of the place they love. Imagine how you'd feel if someone said your husband or wife was 'awful, appalling … lazy, ineffective, ill intentioned and not at all what they were cracked up to be'.

The nature of life being what it is in the service sector, you have to bite your lip and say, 'Hey, I'm really sorry you feel like that. That's awful. How can I help you? Of course I'll sort this out for you …' (inside, of course, you are saying, 'you smug, sanctimonious, illiberal, ignorant bastard').

It's not easy, is it?

Lesson: For Peter, getting the people thing right is virtually all there is to this.

Training staff properly, helping them to lift their game, creating an ambience of total self-confidence and enjoyment, keeping them looking forwards are the things that will help you be better than the next place.

Yet this wasn't quite how it started out.

In 1972 Peter Lederer packed his bags and left Britain for good. Like John Neill of Unipart, he was in despair about the place and believed it was truly impossible to build a career anywhere so utterly lacking in decent labour practices, that was completely devoid of any sense of what 'good' was. No one ever complained in the 1970s. We tolerated double-digit inflation, Wimpy Burgers, Des O'Connor, Sköl Lager, Jefferson Airplane and the Wilson/Heath now-you-see-them-now-you-don't political charade. Do you remember a wine called Bull's Blood? Do you remember Pomagne? Do you remember Smash and Marvel and Double Diamond and Mothers Pride? No wonder Peter fled the UK. It was truly dreadful. Me? I was in love so I stayed and put up with it.

He, on the other hand, went to the USA where they welcomed him warmly and then told him he was very lucky because he qualified for work and one other thing – conscription to fight in Vietnam. He thought about this carefully for a few seconds before leaving to work in Canada.

Lesson: Don't fight other people's wars.

His career in Canada was fulfilling. The Four Seasons, the Plaza. Hotels where systems were sharp, people counted (customers, staff, everyone), training was taken seriously and the quest for improvement was constant. Vietnam over, he went back to the USA and says that in the North American continent as a whole there was a real sense of what 'good' was and how to achieve it. The sloppy amateurism of the UK didn't compare.

And it still doesn't.

Yes, we've caught up – we've had to – but not everywhere and not convincingly. We still don't really understand how to hire, how to coach and how to treat people. UK human resources departments are way behind their US counterparts in the standards they set and in the importance with which their disciplines are regarded.

Lesson: Getting your HR operation right may be the biggest thing you'll do.

The lure of running Gleneagles brought Peter back in 1984. This old British Rail hotel was tired, nostalgic and rudderless. Like an old cruise liner it celebrated times past but was some way off being a great or even very good hotel of the late twentieth century.

A slow, steady process of improving its self-confidence started with the crisis of having three different owners in the first twenty months. But crises, like the prospect of imminent execution, concentrate the mind wonderfully. It helped Peter to *focus* staff on their mission of improvement in a way that a calmer environment might not have done. *Crisis creates Dunkirk spirit. Dunkirk spirit creates huge productivity.* And so it was.

Lesson: Create a crisis to create momentum and purpose.

Gleneagles also had to change its customers. Looking after your core customers and recruiting new ones at the same time is in the mood of the moment at places like Marks & Spencer. It takes a skilled marketer to juggle the loyal old with the inquisitive and potentially dismissive new clientele.

Lesson: The customer may be always right but you've got to work constantly to get the right customers.

You need to surprise them, not just give them what they *say* they want. *You've got to educate your consumers if you want to stay ahead.* Chicken Kiev was a big surprise to 1970 consumers in the UK. Who thought Starbucks could get away with so much money for a coffee? A film about the last days of Christ's life will never make any money. (Sorry Mel, I know you're keen on it but it just won't work.) But of course it did. Triumphantly.

Life in a successful business involves the CEO constantly redrawing the horizon, nudging his lieutenants and saying, 'Hey, look at this ... fancy a trip to see what the next mountain is like?'

Sir Peter Bonfield, ex-CEO of BT, used to say it wasn't about looking at the next horizon, it was about getting high enough to see the horizon beyond the horizon beyond that one.

Peter is obsessed with 'S' curves, wakes at night screaming, 'Where are we on the curve?' And he's right – for leaders to be a step ahead they have to know where they are at any given moment in time.

Question: Do you really know where you are?

If the 1980s was about the *physical* stuff and the 90s was about *quality*, which meant getting the people right – people from new environments such as engineering, fast-moving consumer goods, retailing, people who brought in new ideas, people who were great at systems but were not just systems people – then the twenty-first century's first decade is about *innovation*. 'Same old' won't do any more.

Because if you aspire to be the best you create a huge problem for yourself.

Lesson: Being best means constantly having to get better just to stand still.

You set up the benchmark for your competitors, who catch up quickly. You even train their next-generation managers. Guess where they are going to recruit their new stars from?

You satisfy your customers, who want it even better next time. Succeeding is a progressive thing – like the times of an Olympic runner. Being as good as you were last time out isn't good enough.

And everyone measures everything at the top end of the market on a global basis. No excuses for being less good in Romania even if it's a bit quaint there. The world today is one stage. There is one set of Oscars and you are up for one every time you open your doors to a new or an old customer. *All customers are mystery shoppers nowadays.*

The pace of change is accelerating so dramatically it's hard to spot it. Especially sitting in the serene isolation of Auchterarder where it's sometimes hard to know just what's going on in Rio or Shanghai that might alter the way the world is regarding your offering today.

Lesson: Constantly try to see yourself as others see you.

There was a time when working in a hotel was perhaps not the greatest job. No longer does it sit below the military and the Church as a place for your offspring to go. It's no longer a stepping stone or a vacation job: it's a career, and it's an important one. Leisure and service are big. In May 2004 Gleneagles received 400 applications for jobs, which tells you a lot.

Success is always a smile away in this business. Unlike some hotels, Gleneagles has always had a theatrical bravado about itself. It feels young and experimental, but also has a sense of having been there for-ever. It is characterized by an ability to break moulds and to do the unusual. The corridors are littered with dead sacred cows.

Peter is living proof that crucial to real success is a mix of modesty and an appetite for achievement. He remains excited by what he does and by the new things they keep on coming up with. His epitaph would be: 'For whom the next horizon was never enough.'

So what is the next horizon? A bit like asking Mel Gibson. Whatever else we can guess, it won't be dull.

Lesson: Set up new initiatives and challenges the whole time. You may not always get it right, but you keep people on their toes.

17 The Loneliness of Leadership

Being a real business success like a CEO can be lonely – success often makes you remote from the real world. The route to real success is to avoid this at all costs.

'all you need in this life is ignorance and confidence. Then success is sure'

Mark Twain – letter to Mrs. Foote 1887

'The trouble with fulfilling your ambitions is you think you will be transformed into some kind of archangel and you're not. You still have to wash your socks.'

Louis de Bernières, The Independent 1999

IN PRAISE OF LEADERSHIP

I was talking about success to John Triggle, who used to be CEO of Spalding Worldwide. He pondered for a while and said,

> *'I'm quoting someone, apologies for not remembering who, but it was about the appeal of craftsmanship, which is in a way the real mark of success. This anonymous person said, "Watching a champion breadslicer would capture my attention. A champion anything would do."'*

It's all about getting really accomplished at something. It's like that moment when you start *thinking* in a foreign language – that kind of level of mastery equals success.

John also told me a story about his early life. He was a bright child, *'and I dreamed of becoming an architect when I was a teenager ... but I began to develop a scientific bent and found I was good at it ... so the dream changed to wanting to be a brain surgeon ... all that power of good from being deft ... but I discovered you needed Latin to be a doctor, which put me off ... so I settled instead for being a good chemist. When I got a job at Pfizer I told my boss the story about really wanting to be a brain surgeon. "No you didn't," he told me, "if you'd really wanted to be a brain surgeon, really, really wanted it, you'd have done the Latin. You got what you actually wanted. Chemistry." '*

Lesson: Your inner urge is stronger than your rational self.

It follows that success will happen to those who need it – the drive will take them there. In the USA they seem to have more appetite than we do. For everything. The American Dream is hungry stuff. Hence their bigger wallets, bigger bodies, bigger everything.

John is a good-humoured man, who said,

'Do you know, I've never felt lonely. Alone, yes, but never lonely. And if I felt things weren't quite working out I thought that was my problem and no one else's.'

Never being lonely is a mark of some success in life.

Loneliness is a problem many CEOs suffer from – no one to talk to or confide in, no shoulder to cry on, just a remorseless stream of plaintiffs coming in through that open door. Richard French used to say, 'Someone has to motivate the motivator,' then he'd take his team to a wine bar. Motivation in a glass. He *absolutely* refused to be lonely (that's why he was a good leader), and kept everyone going by the power of his self-belief. But for most CEOs it's different.

Increasingly, leaders are creating a more collegiate style – Amy Armstrong (Head of Ufi London), Roger Alexander (senior partner of Lewis Silkin, the legal firm) – people who believe in extracting the maximum 'people value' from what they do.

Success is elusive.

Unless, of course, you have that calm certainty a few bright young people have when they know no fear and the living is easy. Most CEOs aren't so lucky. They already have the scars of battle.

For many, success is surprisingly hard to define absolutely and probably easier to attain. The so-called successes, people who are exceedingly rich, for instance, are often asked if they are ever satisfied. Nearly all of them say 'No'. It was one of the Rockefellers who, on being asked when he would feel rich enough, replied, 'When I can get one dollar more.'

Because regardless of talent and achievements, regardless of success, we all have to be told we are successes if it is to mean anything.

See the CEO speak at a conference when no one says to him (or her), 'Well done' – because you don't want to be obsequious, because he's too busy, because he's always great so he (or she) must know it without you saying so. But watch his brow furrow as he stands alone and wonders, 'Was I a success or was I crap? Why doesn't anyone say anything to me?'

One CEO practised a management policy of praise by omission. Unusual, eh? Yes, he'd say nothing if you were great and tear you to pieces if you exposed the slightest defect. 'The greater applause', said Triggle, who worked for him at Smith Kline & French, 'was silence.'

The need for praise is deep-rooted. I once heard Tony O'Reilly at the Marketing Society. Brilliant speech. Much applause (absolutely no silence). A few days later I met him at a Heinz event and said, 'Saw you at the Marketing Society. Thank you. You were marvellous.' Twice during the course of the day he passed me and said, 'So I was ok – was I really?'

For most of us, success is that simple. But applause and praise is only part of the story. And it can be dangerous. Don't believe what the critics say, respond more to your own 'inner critic'. Be true to yourself, to your values. Accept the loneliness of power as a penalty of success, but never accept the absence of stimulation and learning. Never let them take away your sense of curiosity.

Without those things, success isn't worth having.

18 People Make the Difference

The way to succeed is to think about people the whole time. Why you should love your customers. Why you can't buy success. How you can polish your business so you maximize its success.

Roger Alexander

'It's sobering to consider that when Mozart was my age he had already been dead for a year.'

A young Tom Lehrer 1978

IN PRAISE OF YOUR WONDERFUL PEOPLE

The lean, chiselled features of a legal professional, that seasoned and battle-scarred veteran of the legal circuit, Roger Alexander, senior partner of Lewis Silkin, wonders briefly if you *can* buy success: 'Look at Chelsea … from zeros to … well, almost heroes'

Money talks, to be sure, but you can't buy this elusive thing any more than you can buy beauty if you're a girl. Money can help you look better but it can't reformulate. It's no substitute for talent and hard work.

What money does create is that 'va va vroom' that can be so exciting. You feel it in a big (or small) successful business or in a city on the move with investment – London, Leeds, Manchester, Birmingham – in all of them. You can feel it as you see the cranes reaching up and rebuilding.

Money puts a sparkle on the shabby. New coats of paint cost money. Money creates momentum.

Lesson: Don't deride the effect that money can have – especially if it's well spent. No one likes a spendthrift but everyone likes a shrewd investor.

Back to Roger Alexander (by no means as wrinkled as I inadvertently make him sound – 'battle-scarred' is a compliment, Roger, honestly. You really are like Brad Pitt in *Troy*). As a lawyer, he is very conscious of the litigious world in which we live and the disconcerting truth spoken by one of his competitors intent on preserving their success:

> '*My priorities nowadays are: 1. Our reputation; 2. Protecting ourselves against the client; 3. Doing the job.*'

Protecting themselves against the client – has the world gone completely cynical and mad?

In Roger's not so much old-fashioned as punctilious world, 'doing the job' was what led to 'reputation' and this protection thing didn't enter the equation at all. Times change, however. Even cricketers wear helmets nowadays.

Lesson: You have to be very circumspect nowadays. Take nothing for granted. Write minutes of meetings. Be careful.

Success? We eye each other beadily. I know Roger is incapable of letting anything sloppy or ill thought through pass – that's why he's so good. Like a powerfully built trout he rises to the lure before knocking it contemptuously aside, all the while smiling. I like his analysis of a business sector we both know well – advertising:

> '*It's all about people ... always has been ... the relationships they have and the relationships they create ... it's the great people in advertising like Ogilvy and Abbott and Hegarty who create this rock-solid culture.*'

As Jim Collins said in *Good to Great*,

> '*get the wrong people off the bus and the right people on it and you may have the chance of building a decent business*' (or words to that effect).

We are talking to Neville Abraham, restaurateur, entrepreneur famed for Chutney Mary, Chez Gerard and many others who, on being asked what he would do if he started again, says firmly, 'I'd ignore my career and I'd go travelling to as many places as I could.'

What we all agree is that the urge to go plural is indulged at the wrong end of life. The best lawyers and the most accomplished executives all have and definitely need breadth of experience, need to have done lots of things. In the end it isn't until you've tried lots of different things that you really know what you want to do. Career planning isn't a simple step-by-step process that follows two-dimensional, headhunter logic.

Lesson: As a potential employee – have the courage to experiment and keep your mind and eyes open. A career should not be like a lead weight: it should be an exhilarating, learning experience.

Lesson: As a potential employer – the day you stop being a 'people person' is the day you'll stop having the prospect of success. Encourage people to spread their wings, not to be myopically focused.

Lewis Silkin is a substantial business employing 120 lawyers but, in the modern world, not a premier division legal player. It focuses on the media, creative and high-tech sectors. It is not a supermarket. More Fresh 'n' Wild on a large scale.

Its success is that it is highly rated by those who know it in the 'leave your wallet with them and it'll be fine' sense. Masses of integrity, sharp, bright, client-focused people – a real brand that does its work in a very distinctive way. People who work there seem to like it a lot. They also agonize over how they present themselves and how what they do comes across.

As a rule I am a profound sceptic of those modern-day magicians of marketers who describe everything that moves as a brand. There are very few of these things – what great brands have is a total consistency of delivery and behaviour and the power to sustain, despite the mismanagements and catastrophes life throws at them. Great brands are marques, like Heinz, John West, Perrier. They stand for values that an architect has crafted and embedded into their DNA. They are big enough to be able to say 'Sorry' and for people to believe them.

Money can help, but no great brand does what it does just for money.

Lesson: If you want to build a brand take your time, hold your breath, tell the truth and be unfailingly consistent.

Roger has built a brand at Lewis Silkin – one of the very few in this sector. The people there all live and breathe his values. They have a certain kind of feistiness, protestant work ethic, a sense of humour, good manners and kindness – odd word for lawyers, but true for Lewis Silkin. And one other thing: Roger would rather be remembered for his work than his wealth – unusual in the twenty-first century.

So does he have any view of what his corporate epitaph might be? 'I'd like to make Lewis Silkin a place where people want to work and where clients want to come.'

I think he might have added that great line of the banker J. P. Morgan: 'Our clients' belief in the integrity of our advice is our greatest asset.'

Roger's credo sounds not unfamiliar (I can't really imagine anyone wanting to create the opposite), but I think he misses something that marks the place out in a very distinctive way: they are very good and very nice and very normal and very interesting and *don't take themselves too seriously.*

Lesson: Not taking yourself too seriously makes people value the integrity of your advice because it seems to be for them and not for you.

I like Lewis Silkin because they have mahogany values packaged in modern art. I think they are old-fashioned trendies, a bit like Morrissey fans. But I also think they have the great benefit that the best of the specialists and boutiques also have – Europa in investment banking, BBH in advertising – integrity, appetite, a reluctance to play a corporatist game and *an absolute refusal to do anything just for the money.*

When you have such a clear set of beliefs and a clarity of purpose about being honest, life gets easier. The truth is a powerful weapon, especially if delivered in a confident way.

Roger was not involved much, as far as I know, with Lord Denning, but he could have written his pupil master's remark, 'People employ us for our certainties, not for our doubts.'

And Roger has no doubt that success is fun, that money helps, but that the face that stares at you in the mirror every morning had better be honest or none of this is worth a candle. Success, he believes (and I know him well enough to be certain of this), is how you feel about yourself and how confident you are that you can give the very best counsel to people and being honest enough to recommend someone else if you really think they can do a better job. Beyond that, it's being certain that this message is understood and delivered by your people and that you teach them how to deliver it every single time.

Lesson: Being comfortable that you are doing your best for your customer makes you good at what you do.

I suppose the trouble with most lawyers is that the concept of success seems alien to their being. They just are. They often tend to make their money from disaster – litigation – or necessity – employment, conveyancing issues and so on. When the economy's terrible they make money from insolvency, and when it's good from start-ups and M&As. The world at large doesn't much like lawyers – rich predators. *Plus ça change* since Chaucer's time. Yet 'success' seems a reasonable word to attach to a business enterprise that values its customers and its values so highly.

Lesson: You don't have to be a bastard to win.

19

There's More to Life than Success

Do I really need to succeed? Does it matter? Or am I being seduced into being another wage slave? Thriving executive or beach bum? Good contemporary Generation 'Y' stuff – it's your call – this is a dilemma of those who are most likely to succeed.

Deborah Lewis and Rebecca Davis

'... *to achieve it (success) one only has to be cunning.*'

Mikhail Lermontov. A Hero of our Time

'*Success? I don't believe it has had any effect on me. For one thing I always expected it.*'

Somerset Maugham – written in 1908

IN PRAISE OF YOUTH

What follows smacks of stereotyping, but a point needs to be made about young people that I see made too infrequently. Young Britain today has a certainty about right and wrong, about good and bad, that Old Britain lacked. This is a caring generation. Their contempt for politicians is pretty intense. Their attraction to bringing up families, to putting stuff back into society, to the environment, to self-improvement, seems entrenched. They are into self-improvement, and they can see through the marketing chicanery. And yet they are quite old-fashioned. Recent research shows that a massive majority are proud of being British, approve of the Queen (not Charles, poor chap, who is a kind of pantomime loser in their eyes), disapprove of the Euro and have a splendidly sensible attitude to the work/life balance.

As regards success, what is so bizarre is their calm certainty that material success is not especially difficult. They do truly live in the post-Saatchi world where 'anything is possible'.

A goddaughter of mine, Rebecca, is extremely bright – a 14-year-old at St Paul's Girls' School who even in that exalted establishment wins form prizes and big, signature prizes like the Monica Dickens for creative writing. Not only is she very bright, she is also very nice and mature beyond her years. I took her out for lunch recently and asked, 'What do you think you'll end up doing as a career – it's a rotten question, but I'm interested in whether you've thought about it.'

She smiled. Remember she's fourteen.

'Yes. Of course I have. Given where I'm being educated, after I get my degree most people might expect me to go into investment banking or corporate law or something like that. I rather think I'll go into fashion design or fashion media, which I really like and for which I think I have some talent. I won't earn as much, of course.'

She has no thought of Mammon, but has a clear sense of focus on career satisfaction. She is a paradigm of the age.

'Success' seems to have confused and stymied a lot of very bright people. To some it's simple, to others, such as Deborah Lewis, a Mars Graduate Trainee, class of 2003, it isn't. Deborah is bright and piercingly focused. To her friends she is known to be intolerant of fools. It's a fault, they tell her. Unsurprisingly, hardly any of her friends are fools. Yet success is a difficult topic.

She is uncharacteristically tentative because, as she puts it, 'There's this confusion between happiness and success. The two are seemingly separate and quite subjective.'

They *are* quite separate, sure, but many get happier if they are successful and most certainly unhappy if they are unsuccessful.

She described all her conscious moments of success as 'moments of achievement' – getting into Cambridge, into Mars, into the Holst Singers. Lots of hard work paying off. When it happened a sensation of elation overwhelmed her – briefly. I privately speculate on the success sensation as resembling an orgasm (not that Deborah herself would have said this – much too well brought up), but clearly success cannot be a constant state of sensation like that – even by *When Harry Met Sally* standards, this sounds too exhausting.

Deborah confesses that through school and university she thought career was everything. Now, deeply embedded in the heart of one of the world's most successful companies, she is beginning to think there's more to the work/life balance, with the balance not being so aggressively tilted to work (although being a good Mars girl she's still got a nose-to-the-grindstone mindset). It's because she's thinking like this that she has a real chance of becoming a successful, consumer-sensitive marketer as opposed to a get-through-that-glass-ceiling bore.

What is success?

Were Mayo and Simpson at Marconi successful? Their personal bank balances would say so. Their reputation until the very end of that fool-hardy escapade on which they embarked would say so. History will probably and surely rightly judge them more harshly.

Superficial success is about 'me', my bank balance, my peerage, my sense of self-esteem.

Real success is about doing stuff for others.

What is success?

This is what Deborah, in common with a lot of her contemporaries, seems to think.

1. It's about *strength of self-awareness* – finding your true strengths and using them.

2. There is *no such thing as failure* because you can always bounce back if you want to.

3. The real measure of success is *creating something from not very much.*

Deborah tells me the story of her great-grandparents who came to Britain from Eastern Europe with nothing. He taught in the East End. Their children all went to university and did well, one became a QC, one an eminent doctor and one deputy chairman of the late lamented GEC. So *they* were successful? Of course, but it was the great-grandfather and great-grandmother who were the true amazing, primal *successes* who created a fire that became an inferno of talent that has now gone through three generations. A good story.

Deborah has a friend whom she is convinced will be an extraordinary success as a tenor. It's down to talent, charisma, timing, luck, but most of all it's down to self-esteem and energy.

You won't make it if you think you're crap. You won't make it if you are crap, either.

Whichever way you look at it, success is appealing. We want to meet successful people because they are usually interesting. But the quest for success in the purely materialistic sense is seen as increasingly inappropriate.

Success is easier to achieve than to define for the Deborahs of this world, I reflect, as I say goodbye to a star of the future, a success waiting to happen. One of the things that seems to mark out successful young people is that they seem to care so much more than previous generations. The world will be a better place with them running it. We are lucky. Believe me.

20 How to Succeed as a Salesman

The sweet smell of success. Sales have never mattered more in our busy, get-results-now world. How to achieve sales success and how to close the sale. This may be the most important chapter in this book.

'...as soon as we start talking about what we can do right rather than bemoaning what has gone wrong, we win'.

Michael Grove
(On Reagan – The Times*)*

IN PRAISE OF SELLING

Ask a salesman about success and they'll tell you it's about three things:

1. *Short term*: hitting your 'number'.

2. *Medium term*: building a sustainable network of contacts.

3. *Long term*: building relationships that will stand the test of time.

From a business perspective that 'number' will vary, but assume a salesman is selling £1million of product a year. People who can command sales of that magnitude are in big demand. They generally get nice cars – important because of what this says about them to their peers or to their friends. No – you are not what you drive, but it does make a statement about how well you are doing. And if they are young (so many in this Byzantine marketplace are relatively mature) then to progress to the next stage of their career, to a *leadership role* in management ... well, that really matters.

Not that there's anything wrong with sales, just that directing, managing or leading sales strategy is that much more demanding and rewarding.

Success at its simplest is a big shiny car that has a wow brand name – BMW, Mercedes, Jaguar. Include some toys for the boys – multi-stack CD, air con, TrafficMaster, sports seats, leather trim, 'M' Series, alloy wheels, and you have a very happy operator inside it, be they male or female. Toys appeal to the child in all of us. It amazes me that more firms don't trade on *the psychology of stuff for the car*. Alloy wheels are worth more than what they cost to their owner. *For most salesmen, their car is their office.* They spend more time with it than they do with their partner, so let's make it a sexy office. *Make it an office of which competitors' salesmen are really envious.*

Success is *reputation*. Success is the *significance* with which you are regarded.

It's tangible. Measurable in pounds sold and in bling for the salesman.

Success is BMW, Palm Pilot, Armani, Callaway, the Maldives, Bally, Mont Blanc, Rolex.

Failure, on the other hand, is less tangible. It's soggy, depressing stuff, like drizzle when you've gone out without a coat or umbrella. Loss of reputation. Loss of respect. Loss of stature.

Failure is to miss out. On targets, on sales, on rewards, on acknowledgement.

Failure is expressed in minuses and gloom.

Salesman are driven by their egos and by their customers' loyalty and respect. They *own* their customers. They are the tangible face of their company. In my experience the things that mark out the *successful salesman* are as follows:

1. Planning

Spend a long time on it. Be the quiet champion planner.

Plan the *geography* of your territory.

Plan the 'what's going to happen next?' scenario in your particular context – if you're in B2B then via town halls, planning permissions, local papers, word of mouth, the local Rotary, Round Table, Lions, whatever.

Plan *who's growing*, who's slowing down among your customers.

Plan your week, your month, your year.

Plans – setting them rigorously, working to them and reviewing and revising them – are key.

2. Getting on with people

No, don't be a brown nose, but *like* people – they *are* likeable (nearly all of them) – share jokes, laughs, ideas with them … listen to them … help them (or try to) be *alive*.

3. Know your clients and all your stakeholders

Their problems and opportunities. Know what's on their agenda. Know their business issues really well. But also go beyond that. Know all about them. Their family. Their likes and dislikes. Their hobbies. Their birthday (you don't send them a birthday card? Shame on you).

4. Know your own products backwards

Know every little wrinkle. How they are made – exactly. How long they take to make. What goes into them. Who designed that bit of distinctiveness each one has. Know the good and not so good things. Know the company history … what failed and why it failed. Be a geek. Be an anorak. Be an *expert*. Know more than anyone has known before. Also, be just as expert about your competitors. Keep on learning more. And learn how to tell great 'stories' about your products. A great sales story is the difference between an order-taker and a salesman.

5. Be an optimist

But be a realist too – no one needs a cockeyed optimist. Plan for the worst – always – but hope for the best and show that you are.

6. Be very, very hungry and unreasonably energetic

If you aren't, then you are wasting the salesman's most potent tool – a belief that anything is possible. You are paid to make things happen, to be the *chosen one* in a tender. To be prepared to move heaven and earth for the most important person in your life – your customer.

7. Make sure that sales is seen as important in your company as it should be

Easy in our sophisticated world of high-tech systems, and concepts like derivatives that many don't understand, to place greater emphasis on things such as innovation, organizational development, leadership courses and to forget that sales and the art of old-fashioned salesmanship can literally make the difference between corporate success and corporate failure.

Much of the above has been derived from talking to and observing great salesmen like Mike Dries of Heinz, Sue Farr now at Chime, Stevie Spring who runs Clear, Ken Deeks who's a Non Executive Director at Argyll, Penny Hunt of Columbo, Nick Horswell founder of PHD and Paul Barratt of Tessera (a young star in the emergence, one of the most together salesmen I've seen).

In the end, the greatest rewards for selling come in being praised for success and having your peers think you are the greatest. All the best salesmen I've known can actually do it – sell, that is – and can then do that magic jump into the *sales close*. Getting the order is the key. Make sure you can do it. This is to sales what putting is to golf. All successful salesmen through repeated success become more accomplished and more self-assured. Practice, as we've said before, does make perfect.

I can think of nowhere else that the impact of success or failure has a more brutally naked impact. You can smell success in sales. It's that strong. The need to succeed is all-powerful. Success and survival are the same thing.

I can also think of nothing else that is more important nowadays. If you aren't selling, whether you are in the City or in retail, you are toast. Everyone is judging everyone else by numbers that are a product of sales. Pay your successful salesmen a lot. Do not let them go. Make sure nothing stands in the way of their success. Successful selling is the number one skill of the twenty-first century.

21 Trumped by a New Formula

When one of the world's rich men talks you listen. It's when you read Donald Trump's book you realize there are too many 'Success' books around right now. I include it because he's successful and, hell, it made me laugh.

'...Young men see visions, old men have dreams.'

Acts 2 v.17

TRUMP THIS

These are some of the Donald Trump tips for would-be successes in his book *Trump: How to Get Rich*. Before you (or I) get too dismissive – after all, who do you know that's successful and called Donald except for a duck? – let's hear what he has to say.

1. Dress well

That's like that old Cherry Blossom slogan, 'The shine on your shoes says a lot about you.'

2. Be your own financial adviser

Poor advice destroys you. Better destroy yourself than pay someone else to do it.

3. Be paranoid

Who, me? And why are you looking at me like that? Lay off, Donald, but with a name like yours I'm not surprised you're paranoid. He goes on, 'If someone screws you, screw them back.'

Wish I'd thought of that one.

4. Avoid shaking hands

It's a medical fact, he says, that this is how most germs are spread. Also avoid kissing (he might have added).

5. Follow your instincts

Be paranoid, look for people to screw and don't shake hands, I suppose.

6. Pay attention to the details

Know every aspect of what you are doing. *But I suspect Donald knows what he's on about here – detail is king in retail and everything.* A serious point – whoever you are, stick close to reality; do not be a vague 'I don't deal with detail' person because if you are you won't succeed.

7. Get a prenuptial agreement

Do what? Be paranoid, Donald, and don't shake hands or any of *that* stuff. So if the prenup is solid they can't do you for non-consummation.

22 Success – the Top Tips

Success is a natural thing to aim for so why get confused by it?

This chapter seeks to keep things good and simple so you can put the book down and say 'tomorrow I'm going to set myself my own success programme.'

And then just as you relax I slip in a quote from T.S. Eliot – T.S. Eliot!

'Success is relative. It is what we can make of the mess we've made of things'.

T.S. Eliot

THE SHORT CUT TO SUCCESS (if you hate reading books like this)

Success is whatever you want it to be – no, really, its that simple.

If you are a happy teacher with pupils who are doing well, then you are a great success. If you are a taxi driver who enjoyed doing the knowledge and loves driving, then you are a success.

If you are a millionaire who has just got divorced and who is bored with what he's doing and who has a reputation for being bad tempered and erratic, then I want a word with you. You need help. You are not a success.

Whatever you do, do not do it just for the money.

Whatever you do, do it because you are engaged by it and feel you have some talent at it.

Whatever you do, do it fully and positively and as well as you can.

Whatever you do, try hard to change the things that make it work less well.

Accentuate the positive, eliminate the negative. That's what brings results.

I've spent a lot of time in this book writing about maintaining a positive frame of mind. This is a business book, not a piece on the philosophy of life, but it gets hard to separate the two. It seems to me that if you aren't having a good time, and if what you are spending your working life doing doesn't have the potential to fill you with enthusiasm and excitement, then I can't really help you to be a real success. But then again, you probably wouldn't have bought the book if it had been entitled *How to Get Slightly Better.*

So start by asking yourself if you are doing the right thing. Is it what you want to spend your life doing? Is it fun? Is it fulfilling? Is it what your best friends think you should be doing? How do you feel on Monday morning? Good question, this one.

Then, if the answer is yes, this is a perfectly reasonable way to spend your life with the potential to give you money and pleasure, ask yourself these questions: Am I working hard enough? Am I looking out for opportunities to do things better? Am I progressing fast enough? How can I help those around me do better? Am I laughing enough? Am I full of energy? Do I have the appetite to win?

Feel good about yourself and comfortable in your shoes, and there's a pretty fair chance that you'll be a success. But what it really needs is your own 'Success Programme'. I've given you a long menu to choose from. Here are some of the highlights for you to think about before you create that.

☆ Think about doing yourself justice rather than success.

☆ You are almost certainly much more talented than you'd ever imagined. It's your duty to make the most of these talents.

☆ Succeeding gives you a buzz – go on, you know it does.

☆ Money matters. If you have it you have choice. But never be ruled by money. It's a means to an end, not an end in itself. The cliché that you can't take it with you when you go is true.

☆ Doing things you believe to be worthwhile will make you feel and be successful.

☆ Flex your muscles. Try new things. Do stuff you didn't think you could do. Get out of dozing in your comfort zone. It's a bad place to be because you can never get better there.

☆ You can't succeed in anything unless you have a plan and unless you set yourself milestones.

☆ 'If it doesn't matter who wins, why do we keep score?'

☆ You need to succeed without taking yourself too seriously.

☆ Failure is a great teacher. Don't be frightened of it. Don't blame others when it happens. Learn to succeed by curing failure.

☆ Learn to see things from every point of view. But remember, the key to spectacular, breakthrough success is turning a convention upside down.

☆ You fail not by being stupid but by not being smart enough to keep alert.

☆ Avoid people who are negative thinkers. If they can't be bothered to be optimistic and positive you have to get rid of them from your life. Life is too short to be gloomy.

☆ Learn new things every day. Write them down. You'll forget them otherwise.

☆ Do more than you think you can. Not just work. Everything. Friends, family, hobbies, theatre, cinema, concerts, charity work (and you are allowed to go to the pub as well).

☆ Give other people the credit. Stop trying to own success.

☆ Be obsessed with detail. It sounds unfashionable, but in today's world you really can't leave anything to chance.

☆ See if you can spot patterns. This is called seeing woods as well as trees. Big pictures always comprise shapes. If you can see relationships and shapes you can almost certainly see opportunities.

☆ Feel good. If life isn't fun it should be. Laughter is good for you, as is human company. Most people are nice, try hard to succeed and are great to be with.

☆ Learn to present like a superstar. Read *That Presentation Sensation* that Martin Conradi and I wrote. Do not be amateur in your preparation for a big stand-up show such as a sales conference. Would you employ an amateur surgeon?

☆ Work on your voice. Make it resonate. Enjoy the sound of it. Successes have to talk a lot.

☆ Have the courage of your convictions. Know what really matters in your life. Do not compromise on things you believe in.

☆ Look after yourself. Diet. Sleep. Holidays. Look at yourself. Trim up. Try to do yourself justice. Fat and florid is not in fashion.

☆ Be ambitious for success. And as you reach a new level of excellence force yourself to a new level. Good is not good enough. Better is better. Best is safer until someone else makes a breakthrough. You have to keep on improving.

☆ Get things done. Complete tasks, don't be a finicky must-get-it-perfect person. Done well and on time is good. Done brilliantly but late is not.

☆ Don't let emails rule your life. Clear them properly on a regular basis, using great discipline and rigour. They are a tool.

☆ Deal with your emails promptly and courteously – don't waste time agonizing over them.

☆ Be very cautious what you say in emails and how you say it. Never relax your guard. Realize if it ever got nasty that they could be used in evidence against you. This is not private correspondence – it's very, very public.

☆ Behave yourself. No success of the future will be accused of or vulnerable to accusations of sexism, racism, ageism or bullying (a form of modern management technique I especially abhor), in fact any kind of non-PC attitude. This is the twenty-first century. Grow up.

☆ Don't be a 'binge worker' – someone who is proud to be permanently knackered.

☆ But do have loads of energy. Be more energetic than those around you. It may be pathetic, but being able to last longer and do more with enthusiasm is success vocabulary.

☆ Add interest to all you do – splashes of colour. It will make you memorable and your communication more successful. Being dull is a capital offence.

☆ Read lots. Most people don't nowadays. Read the papers. Read books like this. Earn the reputation of a well-informed and curious person.

☆ Keep things simple. Too much of today is full of unnecessary complication. Start everything with the proviso you aren't going to 'complex it up'.

☆ Get things done. You are paid to do things, not talk about them. In a results-driven world this should be fairly obvious.

☆ Build great teams. Be assiduous at discovering magic chemical mixes – who works well with whom. Find people who make you feel good, look good and do well.

☆ If you want to create a real energy buzz, create a crisis. A controlled crisis can achieve lots. But don't keep on having them. People will think you are a panic merchant.

☆ Get out and meet people. Visit stores where your products are displayed. Talk to your customers and consumers. Be on the move, not stuck behind your PC.

☆ Keep notes of your meetings. Nothing beats having decent records, however good your memory is.

☆ Spend time with your boss getting to know him or her and what they are looking for. Being aligned with those around you is simply common sense.

☆ First impressions count. So if you are going to meet someone for the first time plan how to make your first impression a positive one. Don't go into your meeting without an agenda, without a point of view and without your best listening ears pinned back.

☆ We often talk about transformation – easier to talk about than achieve. Be patient, it'll take time. More important, establish a sense of momentum before you look for major change to happen. Be patient.

☆ Have a full diary. Do a lot. Very few great successes do little or are lazy.

☆ I'd go further than that, in fact: work a lot harder than you do now. You'll be surprised at the cumulative effect it has. If you think you already work hard I suspect you are being kind to yourself. Most of us do less than we could or should.

☆ Promote yourself. If you don't put yourself about and talk up your prospects, why should anyone else?

☆ Hear what people are saying – don't just listen.

☆ See what is going on – merely having your eyes open is not good enough.

☆ Be kind to yourself. Spoil yourself when you've done well.

☆ Be truthful. Remember, the truth is your strongest weapon and you never have to remember what you said.

☆ Frequently, and with brutal self-honesty, ask yourself how you are doing and what you have to improve. Do this in a 'self-honesty hour'.

☆ Having said that, don't be too introspective too much of the time. Introspection seldom leads to growth and nearly always increases stress.

☆ Think a lot more. Doodle thoughts on a sheet of paper. Improve your confidence by getting your brain active.

☆ Be curious about everything. Do not accept anything at face value. Your most formidable tool is three letters – *Why?*

☆ Create contrasts in your life – great stillness followed by great activity, laughter and fun and seriousness, brainstorming and methodical process.

☆ Be kind to people – they will give you so much more if you are.

☆ When did you last have a makeover? Amazing what new clothes, a new haircut and a healthy spent-time-outdoors glow (don't get a flaky-skin suntan, which is so old-fashioned) can do for the way you feel and are seen.

☆ What have you learned in the past few minutes? Why not? Are you taking notes? Learning is the lifeblood of success.

☆ Try making this your anthem 'enthuse, enrapture, enjoy'. It'll make you more successful and even if it didn't you'd be much better company.

☆ Become an expert at something you know you can get good at. It could be Renaissance art or crazy golf. It's just that there's something really impressive and interesting about any kind of expert.

☆ You must always get better, whoever you are, however old you are. If you aren't getting better you are probably getting worse. Think about that one very carefully and then have a 'self-honesty hour'.

☆ Decide when you need to move on from everything you do – hopefully not your marriage or family. The emancipating effect of knowing that you have an exit plan will be extraordinary. Worst of all in life is to be stuck on a same old treadmill.

☆ Use powerful, descriptive language. Avoid sloppy words like 'nice' or 'fine'.

☆ Don't try to be original. Try to be good at what you do.

☆ The real skill is in distinguishing yourself enough but not so much that you stand out on a limb. Too many 'unique' businesses are difficult to pigeonhole, and in consequence very hard to buy from because you have no reference point for what they are selling.

☆ Do everything 10 per cent better, not one thing 100 per cent better. Doesn't sound so sexy, but the overall impact will be greater.

☆ On balance, women have special qualities that men in general lack. Get rid of any glass ceilings in your organization and get your best women in top jobs. Best of all, they are by nature great team builders.

☆ Be true to what you believe. You can't *live* an act. Be prepared to stand up for yourself and to disagree when everyone else says what in your heart of hearts you feel is wrong.

☆ However successful you are, the cudgel of failure can suddenly come out and whack you. Keep on your guard. Don't take your own invincibility for granted.

☆ Develop that urge to succeed, that need to improve – it's what motivates any sportsman, artist or actor, too.

☆ If you don't feel good you almost certainly aren't going to be as good as you should be.

☆ But never be complacent – remember that cudgel.

☆ Getting your people management right is almost certainly the most important thing that you can do.

☆ Only fight your own wars – fight other people's and you'll probably get hurt and get no credit for it.

☆ See yourself as others see you. This means checking out where you are the whole time and where you have met or fallen short of others' expectations.

☆ Set up new initiatives the whole time. It keeps you and others on their toes. New things make you scrutinize the old things. Sometimes you discover hidden virtues in the past and in old products or practices.

☆ Try to enjoy your own company. If you are a leader then you'll spend quite a lot of time by yourself.

☆ Always give those above you honest feedback. Too few do. They'll value you as one of their honest barometers.

☆ Build relationships. This can't be done overnight. Do you have your list of 'the people whose relationship I want to nurture'? If not, do it.

☆ Love your clients, customers, consumers. Without them you are nothing.

☆ If you have a genius working with you who pisses everyone off and doesn't share your values, get rid of them. Life's too short.

☆ Go for specific moments of achievement, for goals. Success becomes real when it is specific and results-focused, not when it's generalized.

☆ You can always bounce back from failure, so never be frightened of failing.

☆ Good salesmen are the true 'masters of the universe'. If you don't hit your sales number you are toast in the twenty-first century.

☆ Planning is one key to sales success. This means that great sales programmes take time.

☆ Other keys are to do with knowing people well, not superficially, and getting on with them. It's not a 'nice to have', it's an essential.

☆ Become a great storyteller. That's what Ronald Reagan was. Good at convincingly telling you how it was with lots of specifics but always keeping it simple.

☆ Knowledge of what you are selling in detail, in every respect, is vital. You can't sell and be vague on the detail.

Most of us want to be a success. But there are those who believe the only way to succeed is to stab others in the back. For me, that kind of so-called success not only isn't important – it's a positive menace that is currently under severe scrutiny. Be a bullying bastard at your peril.

What most of us want is to have been a player, to have achieved something worthwhile, to have given others the legacy of our learning, to have had a great time, to have made some great friends and enough money not to worry about the next holiday.

There's nothing wrong with having a burning need to make things around you better.

The 'tools of success' are contained here. Some won't work for you but some will transform your performance. Create your own tool kit from those that work and then *go for it.*

Action List: The Ten Most Useful Success Ideas I've Found in This Book

01	
02	
03	
04	
05	
06	
07	
08	
09	
10	

Reading List

Dude, Where's My Country? by Michael Moore (Penguin Books, 2004)

The New Alchemists by Charles Handy and Elizabeth Handy (Hutchinson, 2004)

Re-imagine! by Tom Peters (Dorling Kindersley, 2003)

On and Off the Field by Ed Smith (Viking, 2004)

The One Minute Manager by Ken Blanchard and Dr. Spencer Johnson (HarperCollins Business, 2000)

The Rhythms of Life by Russell Foster and Leon Kreitzman (Profile Books, 2004)

That Presentation Sensation by Martin Conradi and Richard Hall (FT Prentice Hall, 2001)

48 Hours to a Healthier Life by Suzi Grant (Penguin Books, 2003)

Five Dysfunctions of a Team by Patrick Lencioni (Jossey Bass Wiley, 2002)

Competitive Strategy by Michael Porter (Free Press, 2004)

The Fifth Discipline by Peter Senge (Nicholas Brealey Publishing, 1994)

The Loyalty Effect by Frederick Reichheld (Harvard Business School Press, 2001)

In Search of Excellence by Tom Peters and Robert Waterman (Profile Business, 2004)

Trump: How to Get Rich by Donald Trump (BBC Consumer Publishing, 2004)

Good to Great by Jim Collins (Random House, 2001)

Stag Hunt by Anthony McGowan (Hodder and Stoughton, 2004)

The Cluetrain Manifesto by Rick Levine, Christopher Locke, Doc Searls and David Weinberger (Perseus Publishing, 2000)

I am Right, You are Wrong by Edward de Bono (Penguin Books, 1991)

Change Activist by Carmell McConnell (momentum, 2002)

Jack: Straight from the Gut by Jack Welch with John A. Byrne (Headline, 2003)

Purple Cow by Seth Godin (Michael Joseph, 2004)

The Tipping Point by Malcolm Gladwell (Abacus, 2002)

A Smile in the Mind by Beryl McAlhone and David Stuart (Phaidon Press, 1998)

Creativity in Business by Michael Ray and Rochelle Myers (Doubleday, 1986)

The Philosophy of Branding by Thom Braun (Kogan Page, 2004)

The Japanese Mind by Robert C. Christopher (Pan, 1984)

The E-Myth Revisited by Michael E. Gerber (Harper Collins, 2001)

Who Moved My Cheese? by Dr. Spencer Johnson (Vermilion, 2002)

GE Workout by Dave Ulrich, Steve Kerr, Ron Ashkenas and Debbie Burke (McGraw-Hill, 2002)

Key People and Companies

Who directly or indirectly made a contribution to this book.

Michael Winner – Film Maker and Columnist
Michael Moore – Film Maker and Author
Rocco Forte – Hotelier
Gerry Robinson – ex Head of Granada
Charles Allen – Head of ITV
Sir Clive Thompson – ex Head of Rentokil
William Atkinson – Head of Phoenix High School
Gerald Ronson – Head of Heron
Tom Peters – Guru
Sir Clive Woodward – ex Head of British Rugby Team
Robin Marlar – Writer and Headhunter
Marjorie Scardino – Head of Pearson
Ian Parker – Head of Privilege Insurance
Ed Smith – Cricketer and Writer
Greg – Customer Service at Argos
Tom Hings – Brand Director Royal Mail
Alan Leighton – Head of Royal Mail
Terry Nagaii – ex Head of Panasonic UK B2B
Bob Gizueta – ex Head of Coca-Cola
Rupert Murdock – Head of Sky et al

Andrew Neill – Broadcaster
Jack Welch – ex Head of General Electric
Sir Fred Goodwin – Head of Royal Bank of Scotland
Jeff Immelt – Head of General Electric
Serge Trigano – Founder of Club Med
Richard French – ex Head of Y&R
Ian Potter – ex Creative Head of FCO
David Abbott – ex Head of AMV/BBDO
Ian George – Head of Pathe Distribution UK
David Ogilvy – late Head of O&M
Suzi Grant – Broadcaster and Writer
John Neill CBE – Head of Unipart
Leo Burnett – Founder of Ad. Agency
Mike Dries – ex Sales Head of Heinz UK
Tersa Ceballos – Marketing Head of Leapfrog UK
Mary Jo Jacobi – Public Affairs Head of Shell
Hugo Robson – Cabinet Office
Martin Conradi – Head of Showcase Presentations
Reinier Evers – Head of Trendwatching.com

Eugene Beer – Director of Kaizo PR

Ken Deeks – NED Argyll Communications

Dr. Roger Lonsdale – ex Tutor at Balliol College

Derek Davis – ex Civil Servant turned Renaissance Man

Leon Kretzman – Guru and Writer

Paul Allaire – ex Head of Xerox

Jill Garett – Mentor and Consultant at Caret

Sue Farr – Head of Chime

Stevie Spring – Head of Clear

Penny Hunt – Marketing Guru

Kerrie Barker – Mentor and Hygienist

Sir Peter Davis – ex Head of Sainsburys, Reed Elsevier, Prudential

Roger Alexander – Head of Lewis Silkin

Dianne Thompson – Head of Camelot

Peter Lederer OBE – Head of Gleneagles and Visit Scotland

Mike Kirsch – Director of Norwich Union

John Triggle – ex Head of Spalding Worldwide

Nick Horswell – Founder of PHD

John Hegarty – Founder of BBH

Mike Horne – Founder of Horne and Partners

Alison Chesney – Head of Shaftesbury Homes and Arethusa

Tim Ward – Founder of Six Sigma Works

Peter Katz – ex Head of Mettoy

Amy Armstong – Head of Ufi London

Tony O'Reilly – ex Head of Heinz

Neville Abraham – Entrepreneur and Restaurateur

Paul Zisman – Co Founder of Europa

Paul Barratt – Sales Star at Gaskell Carpet Tiles

Deborah Lewis – Mars Star

Rebecca Lewis – St. Paul's Girls School Star

Richard Kirsch – York Star

Richard Bolton – Physio Guru and Media Owner